MW00416234

A GIFT FOR

_____

FROM

_____

DATE

_____

Near in the Night

100 EVENING MEDITATIONS ON GOD'S PEACE AND REST

EMILY LEY

THOMAS NELSON
Since 1798

Near in the Night

© 2023 Emily Ley

All rights reserved. No portion of this book may be reproduced, stored in a retrieval system, or transmitted in any form or by any means—electronic, mechanical, photocopy, recording, scanning, or other—except for brief quotations in critical reviews or articles, without the prior written permission of the publisher.

Published in Nashville, Tennessee, by Thomas Nelson. Thomas Nelson is a registered trademark of HarperCollins Christian Publishing, Inc.

Thomas Nelson titles may be purchased in bulk for educational, business, fund-raising, or sales promotional use. For information, please email SpecialMarkets@ThomasNelson.com.

Unless otherwise noted, Scripture quotations are taken from The Holy Bible, English Standard Version®). Copyright © 2001 by Crossway, a publishing ministry of Good News Publishers. Used by permission. All rights reserved.

Scripture quotations marked NASB are taken from the New American Standard Bible® (NASB). Copyright © 1960, 1962, 1963, 1968, 1971, 1972, 1973, 1975, 1977, 1995, 2020 by The Lockman Foundation. Used by permission. www.Lockman.org.

Scripture quotations marked NIV are taken from the Holy Bible, New International Version®, NIV®. Copyright © 1973, 1978, 1984, 2011 by Biblica, Inc.® Used by permission of Zondervan. All rights reserved worldwide. www.zondervan.com. The "NIV" and "New International Version" are trademarks registered in the United States Patent and Trademark Office by Biblica, Inc.®.

Scripture quotations marked NKJV are taken from the New King James Version®. Copyright © 1982 by Thomas Nelson. Used by permission. All rights reserved.

Scripture quotations marked NLT are taken from the Holy Bible, New Living Translation. Copyright © 1996, 2004, 2015 by Tyndale House Foundation. Used by permission of Tyndale House Ministries, Carol Stream, Illinois 60188. All rights reserved.

Any internet addresses, phone numbers, or company or product information printed in this book are offered as a resource and are not intended in any way to be or to imply an endorsement by Thomas Nelson, nor does Thomas Nelson vouch for the existence, content, or services of these sites, phone numbers, companies, or products beyond the life of this book.

The quote on Day 70 about languishing is from the *New York Times* online. Adam Grant, "There's a Name for the Blah You're Feeling: It's Called Languishing," NewYorkTimes.com, April 19, 2021, https://www.nytimes.com/2021/04/19/well/mind/covid-mental-health-languishing.html?smid=tw-share.

ISBN 978-1-4002-3133-1 (audiobook)
ISBN 978-1-4002-3134-8 (eBook)
ISBN 978-1-4002-3132-4 (HC)

Printed in India

23 24 25 26 27 REP 10 9 8 7 6 5 4 3 2 1

To Bryan, my other half. You complete me in so many ways. This book is dedicated to you, my night owl. You have held my hand and loved me down so many paths. For that, I am eternally grateful. I love you.

Contents

Introduction xii

WEEK 01 1

Day 1: Rest for the Weary 2
Day 2: Bedtime Rituals 3
Day 3: Evening Routines. 4
Day 4: Tools for Tonight 5
Day 5: How Are You? 6
Week 1: Reflection 7

WEEK 02 9

Day 6: Lay It Down 10
Day 7: You Don't Have to Fear the Darkness 11
Day 8: A Prayer to End Your Day 12
Day 9: Blooming at Night 13
Day 10: For You, Who Can't Sleep. 14
Week 2: Reflection 15

WEEK 03 17

Day 11: Closed Doors 18
Day 12: God Is Near 19
Day 13: When You're Hard on Yourself, Remember This. 20
Day 14: Honor Your Season 21
Day 15: A Promise Fulfilled. 22
Week 3: Reflection 23

CONTENTS

WEEK 04 25

Day 16: Choosing Each Other 26

Day 17: Throw It Away 27

Day 18: Date Nights 28

Day 19: To Cherish 29

Day 20: To You, with Love 30

Week 4: Reflection 31

WEEK 05 35

Day 21: An Endless Chain of Compromises 36

Day 22: The Fisherman 37

Day 23: Thirty Thousand Feet Up 38

Day 24: Choosing Between Doors 39

Day 25: A Few Still Moments 40

Week 5: Reflection 41

WEEK 06 43

Day 26: A Nest, Not a Bubble 44

Day 27: Sunrises, Songs, and Sleepy Hands 45

Day 28: Dragons and Good Guys 46

Day 29: Tremendous Love 47

Day 30: A Place to Rest 48

Week 6: Reflection 49

WEEK 07 53

Day 31: Happy Place 54

Day 32: Nacho Day 55

Day 33: Standard of Grace 56

Day 34: A Quick Declutter 57

Day 35: Throwaway Days 58

Week 7: Reflection 59

CONTENTS

WEEK 08 61

Day 36: The Altar Call 62

Day 37: Volume Control 63

Day 38: Pay Attention 64

Day 39: Eyes on Your Own Paper 65

Day 40: On Flowers and Weeds 66

Week 8: Reflection 67

WEEK 09 69

Day 41: Perfection 70

Day 42: The Doing 71

Day 43: Progress, Not Perfection 72

Day 44: The Weight of Perfection 73

Day 45: I Am Healing 74

Week 9: Reflection 75

WEEK 10 77

Day 46: On Grief 78

Day 47: Your Grief Counts 79

Day 48: Don't Trudge Alone 80

Day 49: Take His Hand 81

Day 50: Check-In 82

Week 10: Reflection 83

WEEK 11 87

Day 51: The Real Fruit of Summer 88

Day 52: Your Joy Is My Joy 89

Day 53: Unpacking 90

Day 54: 'Tis but a Season 91

Day 55: Midnight Oil 92

Week 11: Reflection 93

WEEK 12 95

Day 56: The Truest of Friends 96
Day 57: Lake Life 97
Day 58: On Pace and Space 98
Day 59: Stargazing 99
Day 60: Living Fully Alive 100
Week 12: Reflection 101

WEEK 13 105

Day 61: Now I Lay Me Down to Sleep 106
Day 62: Rinse and Repeat 107
Day 63: Late-Night Prayer Sessions 108
Day 64: One Small Step 109
Day 65: Live This Season Well 110
Week 13: Reflection 111

WEEK 14 113

Day 66: Step Away 114
Day 67: Growing Goodness 115
Day 68: Pink Skies 116
Day 69: A Prayer for Your Dreams 117
Day 70: Dulling of Delight 118
Week 14: Reflection 119

WEEK 15 123

Day 71: Fanciest of the Fancy 124
Day 72: The Messy Middle 125
Day 73: Fruit of the Season 126
Day 74: One of the Greatest Love Stories 127
Day 75: Poppy Seed Bread 128
Week 15: Reflection 129

CONTENTS

WEEK 16 131

Day 76: He Is for You .132
Day 77: Heroes and Helpers 133
Day 78: Turned Upside Down 134
Day 79: Without Ceasing 135
Day 80: For You, Who Feel Alone in the Night 136
Week 17: Reflection 137

WEEK 17 141

Day 81: When Hurricanes Hit 142
Day 82: On Love and Luck 143
Day 83: Be Patient 144
Day 84: Collecting Words 145
Day 85: Faith of a Child 146
Week 17: Reflection 147

WEEK 18 149

Day 86: When You Feel Stuck, Change Your Ways 150
Day 87: Preparation for Success 151
Day 88: Dear Diary 152
Day 89: Give Your Best Yes 153
Day 90: For You, Whose Work Is Never Done 154
Week 18: Reflection 155

WEEK 19 159

Day 91: Best-Laid Plans 160
Day 92: Together and Apart 161
Day 93: To Love and Be Loved 162
Day 94: Love Is a Choice 163
Day 95: A Trusted Resource 164
Week 19: Reflection 165

CONTENTS

WEEK 20 167

Day 96: Trunks, Bodies, and Tails 168
Day 97: Life-Giving 169
Day 98: Seeking Delight 170
Day 99: Love and Growth 171
Day 100: Near in the Night 172
Week 20: Reflection 173

A Prayer of Gratitude 177
A Benediction 179
Scriptures for Your Evening 181
Evening Routines 183
Emily's Ideal Evening Routine 185
Acknowledgments 187
About the Author 189

Introduction

Because I'm a busy person by nature, it's taken me a long time to love the ritual of drawing the day to a close. I'd stay awake all night working on projects and reading good books if I could. In the evenings, I tend to be like a runner who, after crossing the finish line, needs an extra jog around the track to slow her mind and body. It's tough to come to an abrupt stop after moving so fast all day.

Implementing a flexible, peaceful evening routine tells my brain that it's time to rest, quiet my mind, and give my body a chance to recuperate. But even when I've completed my nighttime ritual and I'm quietly lying in bed with the lights off, sometimes my mind still races. I worry. I make plans. I rethink things I said or did that day.

My anxiety often gets the best of me when it's time to slow down. Over the last few years, I've found it's more important than ever to ground myself in the truths I know for sure. And when the day is done, rooting myself in God's mercy and grace helps me lay down my fears and worries like nothing else.

In mid-2017, after Brady and the twins (then six and two) were fast asleep, I lay down in my bed, twisted the covers into my fists, pulled them up to my face, and cried. The room was dark, and the only sound came from a few stray cars, out late, passing by. For some reason, I was always able to get through the day with a smile on my face (a genuine one, most of the time), with thoughts of the baby I desperately wanted tucked far into the back of my mind, behind my to-do list and nonstop schedule. But at night, when the world slowed down, when the lights dimmed and my tasks were done, there was nothing to hold back those big feelings. And so the what-ifs, the worst-case scenarios, the tears all flowed. The silence from the room we'd deemed "the eventual nursery" was deafening.

Evenings can be like that sometimes, can't they? The worries and fears we're mostly able to ignore during the day tend to rise to the surface in the dark. That niggling medical concern. Financial worries. Aging parents. Relationship challenges. It's hard to outrun those thoughts when the world gets quiet. That night, I knew I could either allow my broken heart to swallow me whole, or I could help my mind travel to a different place, one with a bit of rest and (hopefully) some healing I desperately needed. I found that I could ground myself in truth to get through another night.

I switched on my bedside lamp, opened to a fresh page in my journal, and wrote these four sentences:

God is for me.

God has not forgotten me.

He hears my prayers.

He is near me at night.

If you've ever experienced infertility yourself, you know what the next few months looked like: a roller coaster of emotions. But every night, when the pain began to bubble to the surface, I opened that journal to remind myself what I knew for sure:

God is for me.

God has not forgotten me.

He hears my prayers.

He is near me at night.

These statements held true every night that followed—even during the happy but challenging ones. The sleepless nights with a beautiful newborn baby by my side. The nights when I'd fall into bed absolutely exhausted from the wonderful, yet nonstop work of mothering. The nights when I burned the midnight oil to tend to a growing business.

Whether you find yourself in a season of darkness and grief, or you're simply thirsty for God's nearness to settle you as the day fades, it's my prayer that this book meets you exactly where you are. There are so many places in the Bible where we read of God's nearness. That, in and of itself, is a comfort to me. Because if He is near, He is protecting us. If He is near, He sees what's going on. If He is near, He is listening to our hearts. What comfort.

> The LORD is near to all who call on him, to all who call on him in truth.
>
> PSALM 145:18

> The LORD is near to the brokenhearted and saves the crushed in spirit.
>
> PSALM 34:18

> Let your reasonableness be known to everyone. The Lord is at hand; do not be anxious about anything, but in everything by prayer and supplication with thanksgiving let your requests be made known to God. And the peace of God, which surpasses all understanding, will guard your hearts and your minds in Christ Jesus.
>
> PHILIPPIANS 4:5-7

That they should seek God, and perhaps feel their way toward him and find him. Yet he is actually not far from each one of us.

ACTS 17:27

I invite you to use this book as a foundational piece of your evening routine. Once the kids are tucked in bed, the house is picked up, and the work put away for the day, give yourself the gift of a few minutes of truth and reflection. Use this devotional as your last jog around the track, allowing your mind and heart to focus on God's mercy and grace. At the end of this devotional, I share my ideal evening routine and invite you to think through your own. In addition to this book, you may want to add a Bible, a pretty notebook or journal, and your favorite pen to your bedside table.

I pray you find peace and stillness in the promises that God is never far away, that He watches over you while you sleep, and that His goodness is true in the light and in the darkness, however long the darkness lasts. When the rest of the world seems uncertain and ever-changing, God is the Rock that cannot be moved and never disappears when the daylight fades to night.

Emily

How are
you, really?

WEEK

01

· · · · · · · · · · · · · · · · · · ·

Rest for the Weary

"Come to me, all you who are weary and burdened, and I will give you rest. Take my yoke upon you and learn from me, for I am gentle and humble in heart, and you will find rest for your souls. For my yoke is easy and my burden is light."

MATTHEW 11:28–30 NIV

· ·

Where do you turn when you get overwhelmed? When you've had a really busy day, meetings on top of meetings, calls on top of calls? When the school requests a parent-teacher conference? When the to-do lists just won't end? There are lots of places the world tells us we can look for freedom. In the snack basket, in the wine glass, in the Netflix binge.

I've tested all those options, and though they offer momentary relief from our day-to-day woes, they do nothing for the long term. Is there another option? A third door?

Imagine yourself as a traveler. You've been walking all day. You're tired, you're hungry, you're thirsty, and your backpack is *so* heavy. What do you do? You take off the pack. You set it down and stretch. You feed yourself and nourish your body. And you rest. You listen to your body and give it what it needs.

You may not be on a cross-country trek, but you and the traveler are a lot alike. You're both carrying a lot, which means you both need rest. So the next time you feel weary, set down your pack and listen to what your body *really* needs.

 Do you have a "weary traveler" tool kit? Consider writing down a few ways you can unwind at the end of a long day. Going to bed early. A hot cup of tea. And maybe some journaling time.

Bedtime Rituals

So, whether you eat or drink, or whatever you do, do all to the glory of God.

1 CORINTHIANS 10:31

Bedtime is a peculiar thing at our house. It is something I look forward to . . . and something I dread. I love the special tuck-in time with my children, saying prayers, snuggling with each one individually. But unfortunately, by this time of day, I am also existentially and unequivocally exhausted. I have been known to say a quick prayer around 7:00 p.m. for God to have mercy on my soul and give me patience to do bedtime well (and also to forgive me for wishing I could skip out on my kids' bedtime ritual and just collapse into bed).

Each child has a special way they like to be tucked in, and they have different things they want from Mom and Dad. With me, they want prayers, kisses, snuggles, time to verbally unpack their day, and back scratches. They also have certain phrases they like to say to me, and for me to say back to them (I will never not say, "Goodnight, precious baby" to Tyler because he says, "Goodnight, precious mama" back, and it is the best part of life). And when it comes to Dad, they like to be tossed into bed. That's right—they want to be picked up and tossed into their beds. This elicits howls of laughter from each child and increases my anxiety tenfold because at this point, my children are so amped up. But alas, it is the Ley way of tucking kids into bed. And they fall asleep knowing they are loved and cared for.

What does bedtime look like at your house? If you have children, what does the ritual look like for them? How can you and your people fall asleep each night knowing you are loved?

Evening Routines

*To acquire wisdom is to love yourself; people who
cherish understanding will prosper.*

PROVERBS 19:8 NLT

. . . .

Winding down after dinner can be difficult for the doers. When you work and serve and care for others all day long, it's tough to calm your pace. But I've found that creating an evening routine tells my brain and my body it's time to slow down. In the same way a good morning routine can kick-start your day, an evening routine can help you peacefully draw it to a close.

For me, this begins once dinner is cleaned up, the kids are in bed, and lunches are packed for the next day. I pick up the kitchen and living room (my brain rests better knowing our home and family are prepared for the next day), then dim the lights in my bedroom. I hook up my phone to a charger in my closet (this is key to a focused, calm evening). I turn down my bed and draw a bath. After a good, long soak, I put on my pajamas and go through my nighttime skincare routine. I usually read a few pages of a book before I turn off the lamp and go to sleep. I'm an early bird, so I'm typically asleep by 9:00 p.m.

This is a loose and flexible routine, but the rhythm sends a signal to my brain that it's time to rest.

 Do you have an evening routine? If you don't, what could that rhythm look like for you? Mine has evolved over several seasons of life, but the core pieces of it remain the same: always a picked-up house, a good long bath, and a book before bed. Write out your evening routine, and try to stick with it for a week.

4

Tools for Tonight

*In peace I will both lie down and sleep; for you
alone, O Lord, make me dwell in safety.*

PSALM 4:8

Getting a good night's sleep requires a comfy place to rest and some uninter-rupted time. But I've found there are a few tools that help me achieve a solid eight hours of rest.

A weighted blanket helps my mind and body settle down. I have a small white fan on my nightstand to keep me cool at night. A white noise app on my phone drowns out any outside noises or distractions. And for those evenings when sleep is hard to find, I keep melatonin on hand to help me doze off. Now, are these products necessary for good sleep? No. Do they make sleep better and easier to find? Absolutely.

Maybe it's time to up your sleep game. After all, sleep allows our bodies to heal, recharge, and stave off disease. What might help you achieve better sleep? Do lights outside your bedroom windows keep you up at night? Consider picking up some black-out curtains. Does your dog like to wake you up in the middle of the night? Perhaps he can sleep in the living room. Try to give a few minutes to thinking about what you might need to get more rest—because rest assured, your body will thank you.

*Assess your sleep situation, and consider ways you might support
your body's need for sleep. Would earplugs help? A sleep mask? Could
a free white-noise app help you rest a bit better?*

How Are You?

Think over what I say, for the Lord will give you understanding in everything.

2 TIMOTHY 2:7

I once had a friend who'd often ask, "How are you?" But she never let me answer with, "Fine." Instead, she would gently press, "How are you, *really?*" The answer to that question often looked quite different than simply saying, "Fine."

"I'm tired," I'd sometimes say. "Exhausted, really. I'm not sleeping well. I'm staying up at night worrying about my children." Or sometimes I'd say, "I'm happy. I'm proud of the work I've been putting into a new project. It's taken a lot of dedication, but it's been worth it."

What a gift for someone to be so interested in how we really, truly are. Her practice of pushing me to answer her question honestly is something I've taken with me into all my relationships—most importantly, the relationship I have with myself. It's vital to be honest with myself about how I'm actually doing.

To move forward intentionally, we have to consider where we currently are—which means thinking about how we actually are. So today I ask: How are you? How are you, *really?*

Allow yourself the time and space to deeply, intentionally consider how you're doing and where you are. Lean into that feeling, even if it's uncomfortable. Write it all down. Now, considering how you feel about where you are currently, where would you most like to go?

Reflection

As you close out this first week, I invite you to look at how your evenings may have changed in the past few days. Use this page to reflect on the week, and check in with yourself. Did you make a change in your evening routine? How did it feel to shake things up a little bit?

Are there parts of your evening routine you'd like to change moving forward? Are there things on your heart you want to share with God? I invite you to pause and reflect on this for a few minutes. And, of course, to find some good, comforting rest this evening.

_____

_____

_____

_____

_____

_____

_____

_____

_____

_____

Lazy it all down.

WEEK

02

· · · · · · · · · · · · · · · · · · ·

Lay It Down

Cast all your anxiety on him because he cares for you.

1 PETER 5:7 NIV

. . . .

The evenings can be tough, especially if you're an anxious person like me. I tend to power through my days, but when I slow down at night, that's when my worries and fears begin to surface. But when I fill my well with a little truth, like reading a devotion or reciting a Bible verse, I replace my worries with a bit of calm. And that keeps my mind from racing.

In the past few weeks, during those middle-of-the-night moments when I wake up and can't fall back asleep (because my mind is worrying about tomorrow's to-dos and yesterday's mistakes), I've been hearing these words: *lay it down*. There's nothing I can do about the worries flittering through my brain at 3:00 a.m., so I lay it all down.

When you find your mind clinging to a worry, acknowledge it. Then, just set it down. It will be there tomorrow, when you'll have some time to think about how to manage it. To me, *lay it down* also means *give it to God*. Hand that problem to the One who already knows how tomorrow will go. He'll carry it for you. Right now, it's time for you to go rest.

> *The next time your middle-of-the-night worries keep you up, recite to yourself: "Lay it down." Imagine yourself holding whatever concern or task is on your mind, then setting it down and walking away for the evening. You can pick it up again in the morning if you want.*

You Don't Have to Fear the Darkness

You will not fear the terror of the night, nor the arrow that flies by day.

PSALM 91:5 NIV

Have you ever noticed that monsters seem scarier in the dark? As a child, I'd lie awake at night and worry about each of the shadows in my room. *Is that something scary?* I'd wonder. *Should I be afraid? Am I safe?*

Morning would come, the sun would peek into my window, and my pretty pink room would be free from all the bad, scary things once again.

Why does everything seem scarier in the dark? Because without the light showing the truth of these objects, our imagination runs away with what they might possibly be. Our brains tend to play the what-if game with worst-case-scenarios.

As an adult, I no longer lie awake worrying about the shadows in my room or what's under my bed, but I do worry, *What shoe could drop tomorrow? What illness could be lurking? What could I be doing better?* Then, sure as the sunrise, the morning brings light and truth.

In John 8:12, Jesus says, "I am the light of the world. Whoever follows me will not walk in darkness, but will have the light of life." Jesus invites us to remember that He is the light that shines truth on the darkness of this world. What do you fear in the darkness? What truth is Jesus highlighting for you?

11

A Prayer to End Your Day

I lay down and slept; I woke again, for the LORD sustained me.

PSALM 3:5

A prayer for your evening:

Lord, be with me as I wind down for the evening.

Calm my racing mind, and focus my thoughts on peace and sound sleep. I lay down my worries and fears. Hold them gently while I rest.

Soothe the muscles that have propelled me through my day's journey. Replenish my energy while I sleep. Help my body to find stillness and do the divine, complex work of recuperating before tomorrow begins.

Settle my soul, the passion and heart with which I do my day's work. Be near while I rest. Watch over me with love so that I might rise tomorrow renewed and ready to take on the day.

Amen.

Recite this prayer tonight before you begin your evening routine. Allow God's steadfast love to be a soothing balm as you end your day.

Blooming at Night

The fig tree has ripened its fruit, and the vines in blossom have given forth their fragrance. Arise, my darling, my beautiful one, and come along!

SONG OF SOLOMON 2:13 NASB

Did you know some flowers only bloom at night? As a person with a rather black thumb (seriously, it's nearly *impossible* for me to keep a plant alive), I find this fascinating. I know what you might be thinking: *What do you* mean *these flowers only bloom at night? Don't they need water and sunlight to stay alive?* I know, I wondered that too. But it's true!

Take the evening primrose and the moonflower, for example. Rather than blooming by chance during the night, these flowers purposefully bloom when it's dark so they don't have to compete with other flowers for pollinators. Blooming at night helps them to do their very best work at the time that works best for them.

This has encouraged me during seasons of "burning the midnight oil." There are some seasons when rest looks a little different for me. Instead of my usual 9:00 p.m. bedtime, sometimes I choose to stay up after others have gone to bed to do my work. I'm far less distracted during these hours, and I'm able to accomplish more work in less time than if I'd tried to tackle it during the day with children underfoot and my email constantly pinging.

Like the moonflower and the evening primrose, try to do your work during the time of day that works best for you. And remember, this is only a season. Burning a little midnight oil for a while is not only productive; it can be filled with purpose if it's also balanced with seasons of rest.

For You, Who Can't Sleep

He leads me beside still waters. He restores my soul.

PSALM 23:2-3

· ·

We all struggle to sleep from time to time. Some evenings, I'm asleep as soon as my head hits the pillow. Other nights, I lie awake wondering if it's time to get the oil changed in my car, or I'm trying to remember the last place a kid left their soccer cleats. Sometimes, it's just inevitable.

When you find yourself in that precarious situation, I have a blessing to pray over you in those moments:

> May your body release the tension in every muscle, big and small, one by one. May your hands lie still by your sides or find rest as you tuck them gently under the warm side of the pillow.

> May your breathing slow to a steady rhythm, taking in cool air to calm your spirit. With each breath in, may you find yourself sinking deeper into rest, melting slowly into peaceful sleep. And with each exhale, may you release the worries that have been binding your lungs as calm and comfort wash over you in waves.

> May your heart rest with the assurance that God is standing watch. He, who never slumbers, is keeping guard and protecting your heart, mind, and body while you recover. He loves you. He is for you. Sleep well.

Are you sleepy yet? Give yourself the gift of an early bedtime tonight, even just a few minutes. You are worthy of a great night's sleep.

Reflection

In the evening, when the world begins to slow down, sometimes we find ourselves feeling alone with our worries and concerns. But God is near in the night. What thoughts have bubbled to the surface for you this week as you've leaned closer to God?

_____

_____

_____

_____

Looking back: this week, I've felt _____

_____

Looking ahead: moving into next week, I'm hopeful _____

_____

Looking inward: what's weighing on me is _____

_____

Looking outward: I am hopeful for _____

_____

A prayer for protection: Lord, be near me when _____

_____

You are
fearfully
AND wonderfully
Made – and
you are HUMAN.

WEEK

03

· · · · · · · · · · · · · · · · · · ·

Closed Doors

The Lord is near to the brokenhearted and saves the crushed in spirit.

PSALM 34:18

Many of us carry memories of what might have been or what almost was. A date on the calendar may suddenly trigger a memory of when a door was closed, sometimes gently with a soft goodbye, sometimes with a slam and so many questions left unanswered. What would have been your wedding anniversary. What would have been his birthday. The day she took her last breath and slipped into heaven.

These are the moments that slice into the timelines of our life—marking the before and then the after. Sometimes grief stays by our sides, a dull and nagging pain. Sometimes it appears in bursts, unexpected and unyielding. At times, it lives on the outskirts of our thoughts, tinting our days just a little. Other times, grief is a heavy blanket weighing us down, begging us not to move forward.

Whatever loss you have suffered, however grief shows up in your life, I honor your pain. And I'm holding space for your sadness and your questions with the Lord today.

 Bring your losses, both great and small, to the Lord today. Make space to honor your sadness.

18

God Is Near

The LORD is near to all who call on him, to all who call on him in truth.

. . . .

If you are hurting, feeling as if this particular situation will last forever, remember this: the Lord is near.

If you feel isolated, alone in your pain, remember this: the Lord is near.

If you are knee-deep in the wait, stuck in the messy middle without a fast-forward button, if you feel like hope is a friend who has turned her back on you, remember this: the Lord is near.

If you are aching with want, if you have been let down by one too many Swipe Rights, if you have seen one too many single pink lines, or if you are suffering the loss of what might have been, remember this: the Lord is near.

If you are turning the page on the calendar with a hole in your heart, knowing the day is coming, feeling like your heart is cracked open again every twelve months, remember this: the Lord is near.

Whatever your pain, the Lord shares in it. He is near, and He is close to the brokenhearted.

 Friend, ask the Lord to walk with you on whatever path you're traveling today. I promise you, He's nearby, ready to give you the comfort you're looking for.

When You're Hard on Yourself, Remember This

Let us not become weary in doing good, for at the proper time we will reap a harvest if we do not give up.

GALATIANS 6:9 NIV

Do you have an endless loop of critiques running through your mind? Did you burn the chicken or raise your voice again? Grace isn't for perfect people. Grace is for you and me, who try and fail and keep trying.

> May you receive this blessing of grace upon grace. May you press pause on the soundtrack of "should have" and "Why didn't you?" and "You're so . . ." Remember Who's in charge of your identity. Remember Who is heaping grace into your days, just hoping you'll look up and see it. You are not the sum of your mess-ups. You are not the thing you forgot to do, that person you let down. You are not the bad grade you got, the accident you caused, or the misstep you made. You are fearfully and wonderfully made—and you are human. Capable of wildly fantastic things, reaching incredible heights and achievements . . . and also capable of falling short. Capable of letting down others. Capable of letting down yourself. And so may you receive this blessing. I invite you to dust yourself off, to arm yourself with the truth that you, my dear, are beloved. You are not a failure. You are a warrior.

 Take a moment and breathe in those words. Remember He who created the heavens and the stars and the Northern Lights also created you. The one and only you. So chin up, buttercup.

DAY 14

Honor Your Season

While the earth remains, seedtime and harvest, cold and heat,
summer and winter, day and night, shall not cease.

GENESIS 8:22

· ·

I've had seasons of *no* and seasons of *yes*. For many of us, 2020 was a time of *no*. We had to decline gatherings to honor social distancing. We declined in-person meetings to honor public health. Unfortunately, we said no to in-person church, in-person school, and in-person celebrations, all due to COVID-19.

But then, there are seasons of *yes*. Yes to coffee dates with moms from my kids' school. Yes to volunteering in classrooms. Yes to field trips and grocery stores and walking the aisles at HomeGoods. Yes to speaking at events, cheering on the hometown baseball team, and celebrating holidays with friends.

We know from Ecclesiastes that there is a time and a season for everything under heaven. God designed our world to have equal and opposite seasons. Warm springs follow cold winters. Bright days follow dark nights. And joy almost always, eventually, follows sadness.

So honor the season you're in today. Give yourself permission to be comfortable with your yeses, your noes, your joy, and your sadness. There's no need to rush to the next season. It will come in its own time.

Are you overcome with sadness or worry this evening? Honor that with a cup of tea, an early bedtime, or even a full day in bed tomorrow if you need it. Or are you on the flip side of that season? Bursting with joy, excited for what's to come, delighting in this particular day? If so, spread that love. Pause for a second and feel those feelings. By honoring our season, we honor God who created it all.

A Promise Fulfilled

In [God's] great mercy he has given us new birth into a living hope through the resurrection of Jesus Christ from the dead, and into an inheritance that can never perish, spoil or fade. This inheritance is kept in heaven for you.

1 PETER 1:3–4 NIV

There are three simple words that speak to the magnitude, the sacredness, and the incredible power of who Christ is: *He is risen.* Or, like we say in my church, "He is risen! He is risen indeed!" Jesus said it would be so, and it *was.* He promised He would rise on the third day, *and He did.*

If you struggle with a complicated faith or feel as if you're on the outside of a complex fellowship, take a seat here with me. Some days, it feels like you just need hope. Hope that maybe tomorrow could be brighter. That maybe you wish someone would just come in and save everything. Thankfully—for you, for me, for all of us—Someone has already done that. For what He promised, He has fulfilled. Let grace wash over you, delight stir within you, and mercy cover your heart. For God so loved the world (including you, just as you are) that He gave his only begotten Son, that whoever believes in Him will not perish but have eternal life (John 3:16 NKJV).

He is risen. He is risen indeed.

Are you a seasoned Christian, or are you a new believer? By whatever path you found this home, He's glad you've made it here. Delight in the knowledge that He has made a place for you at His table.

Reflection

We often live life on autopilot, not pausing long enough to recognize God at work in our lives. Allow yourself a few moments to reflect on the last few days. How has God fulfilled His promises in your day-to-day life? Celebrate His goodness in your actual life this week here.

God is for you as you travel this journey.

WEEK

04

· · · · · · · · · · · · · · · · · · · ·

Choosing Each Other

Love prospers when a fault is forgiven, but
dwelling on it separates close friends.

PROVERBS 17:9 NLT

My parents have been married for forty-four years. They met in a college class. My dad offered to take my mom's test up to the teacher's desk, secretly so he could learn her name. As any potential suiter did in the seventies, he found her address and showed up at her door to ask her on a date. (Considering this now, in modern times, gives me pause and a giggle.) She said yes, and the rest is history.

I know their marriage hasn't been easy, but my parents are a shining example of what it means to choose each other over and over again. Every day they take their dog, Daisy, to the park to throw the ball. They walk together. They cook together, taking turns making meals or cleaning up. Now that my brother and I have families of our own, my mom sets the table for two. Placemats, silverware, a napkin folded in half, tucked beneath the same white plates we ate on when I was a child.

My parents value each other through their differences. My dad admires my mom and her love for organizing and reorganizing spaces; my mom tolerates my dad's endless collection of power tools. Through all of life's ups and downs, they've made the decision, over and over, to choose each other. I have to imagine that choice wasn't always easy. And yet here they are, still choosing each other forty-four years later.

This week, if you're married, consider a new evening tradition: before you turn out the lights, pray together with your spouse. Lift up your joys, sorrows, and requests to God. Hold hands while you pray.

Throw It Away

Be angry and do not sin; do not let the sun go down on your anger.

EPHESIANS 4:26

When my husband, Bryan, and I get into an argument—the kind that's going to end in my shutting down and not speaking and his being defensive and not budging from his stance—we have a tradition: we throw it away.

"Throw it away" means we pretend to spit the bad attitude, angry feelings, and sheer stubborn will to be right into our hands and then toss it far away. This act originated during a road trip. I was angry, though I'd forgotten what I was mad about, to be honest. We were headed to a weekend getaway, and neither of us wanted the weekend to be tainted by this silly fight, but our egos and pride were all tangled up in the disagreement.

Bryan rolled the passenger side window down, looked at me, and said, "Sue, throw it away. If you will, I will." (Sidenote: he never calls me "Emily," but that's a story for another day.)

I rolled my eyes and smiled. I pretended to "spit" my pride and anger into my hand and tossed them out the window. He did the same. And then we were fine. Later that night, we talked through the issue again without emotion or ego and came to an agreement.

Sometimes our emotions can cloud an otherwise simple situation. Feel free to steal this tradition. I promise it helps.

 Tonight, let's set aside our pride for those we deeply love. Let's strip our words of sarcasm, anger, and bitterness. Instead, let's value people over talking points. What do you need to throw away tonight?

Date Nights

How beautiful and pleasant you are, O loved one, with all your delights!
SONG OF SOLOMON 7:6

. . . .

The doorbell rings, and I look at the dresses strewn around the floor of my bathroom. I take a final glance in the mirror and head to the door. The babysitter is here, and the kids are thrilled because that means board games galore and a Chick-fil-A supper. The babysitter gets the rundown as I shout to my oldest, "Make sure you lock the door!"

A phone dings with a work email. And another. My husband turns on the radio, a deep dive into a new tech stock. I cringe. But we find our groove. Sister Hazel is on repeat as we hold hands all the way. We're heading to our favorite local spot, where we'll probably be fancy and order dinner *and* appetizers, share a bottle of wine, and talk the *entire time* about the kids who aren't with us.

This is what makes a marriage. Making time to be us, not just "Mom and Dad." Hidden inside our professional, proper, parental selves are Bryan, who drives the Jeep and loves beach volleyball, and Emily, with the long hair and the permanent smile. Our former selves are buried inside each of us—you included.

Marriage is about more than just keeping the familial wheels spinning and raising little ones. It's also about dressing up, tuning in, and reconnecting.

If you're married, try to take some time just for the two of you. Maybe plan a night away. Or, if a night in is more realistic during this season, plan for that. Just the two of you, no distractions, sharing something you love.

To Cherish

Husbands, love your wives, as Christ loved the
church and gave himself up for her.

EPHESIANS 5:25

My dear friend Laura has been married to her husband, Joe, for twenty years. They were college sweethearts and have the most precious love story. The best part of their story, though, is that they met when they were toddlers. And now, twenty years in, they have two careers, three beautiful children, a dog, an underwater lizard, and a house.

Recently, they renewed their vows in the same church where they were married. I asked Laura her secret to staying happily married after all these years, choosing one another over and over again. She told me it's the "to cherish" part from their vows.

Many of us, during our wedding ceremonies, recite the vows from *The Book of Common Prayer*, which, in part, states that we promise to have and to hold our partner "for better, for worse, for richer, for poorer, in sickness and in health, to love and to cherish, 'til death do us part."

All things considered, for most couples, the "to cherish" part may be one of the hardest of the vows to live out. And yet, it's the one that most accurately represents what I think we all hope for in married life: To be protected, cared for, and adored. To be considered carefully and with love in every choice and decision. And, at the end of the day, through all things, held dear.

If you are married, how do you cherish your spouse? In what ways can you draw your thoughts and actions closer to the true meaning of cherishing your partner?

To You, with Love

*Therefore encourage one another and build each
other up, just as in fact you are doing.*

1 THESSALONIANS 5:11 NIV

To you, who are waiting to be loved: may you know the boundless, endless love of a Father who knows your hopes and dreams. May you remember how deeply loved you are by Him.

To you, who are struggling in marriage: may the loneliness you feel be soothed by the promise of forgiveness and grace. May you feel wholeness in this particular season as you wait upon the next.

To you, whose marriage is good: may it ever be strengthened. May your love spill over to others, inspiring unions and fortifying communities.

To you, whose marriage has ended: may you be filled with the knowledge of God's unique and specific care for you. He sees you. He hears you. He is for you as you travel this journey, never alone, always with Him.

In whatever season you find yourself, reflect on God's grace through it all. How has He come alongside you in the best of times and in the most challenging of times? In what ways do you need His loving guidance right now?

Reflection

This week, we focused quite a bit on marriage and togetherness. In whatever situation you find yourself—married, single, widowed, divorced—invite God into that space with you. I often reflect on these words from 1 Corinthians 13:4, which say: "Love is patient and kind." Though those statements are true, that doesn't mean love is always easy. Reflect on the truth of those words.

_____

_____

_____

_____

_____

_____

_____

_____

_____

_____

_____

_____

_____

_____

1. Who do you love dearly, with all your heart?

_____

_____

_____

2. What parts of your relationship (or season) are the most difficult right now?

_____

_____

_____

_____

_____

_____

_____

_____

_____

_____

3. What are your hopes for your current or future relationship?

_____

_____

_____

_____

_____

_____

_____

_____

_____

_____

4. Our relationship with ourselves is so important. How can God help you strengthen one of the most important relationships of all?

_____

_____

_____

_____

_____

_____

_____

_____

_____

Don't forget!

You are doing a
Good job!

WEEK

05

· · · · · · · · · · · · · · · · · ·

An Endless Chain of Compromises

And your ears shall hear a word behind you, saying, "This is the way, walk in it," when you turn to the right or when you turn to the left.

ISAIAH 30:21

Do you ever lay down your head at night and count your worth in the number of projects you finished or tasks you crossed off your to-do list? Do you give your day a grade? *A, B+, C-* . . . or worse?

Maybe you don't measure yourself against your productivity. Maybe it's how many times you felt your frustration bubble up, or the volume of your voice as you asked your kids for the fifth time to get ready for school.

All of those things matter, but they're only part of the picture. What about the scrapes you kissed and bandaged? The chores you set aside to tend to another priority? The minutes you spent gently scratching a little back?

My dad always says life is a seemingly endless chain of compromises. Choice after choice, we make a life. I challenge you today to ask God to guide you as you consider each choice on its own, measured against your values and what you hold dear. Step by step. Choice by choice. At the end of the day, congratulate yourself on making it another mile, holding each decision as a tiny part of a larger whole. And don't forget: you're doing a good job.

 Interrupt your checklist-thinking as you lie down tonight. Consider the choices you've made in your life that make you proud and the outcomes you're grateful for.

The Fisherman

Keep your life free from love of money, and be content with what you have, for he has said, "I will never leave you nor forsake you."

HEBREWS 13:5

One time, I heard a parable about a fisherman lying on a beach with his fishing pole. A businessman approaches him and tells him if he went out on a boat, he could catch more fish, sell them, and be more successful. Eventually, the fisherman could sell enough fish to buy a bigger boat with more nets and catch more fish. And after that, he could sell even *more* fish and have enough to buy an entire fleet of boats. And when the business was big enough, the fisherman could sell it for millions of dollars.

"But why?" the fisherman asked.

"Because then you could retire and spend your whole day fishing on the beach."

This is a very short version of this parable, but it illustrates our modern, unquenchable thirst for more, and bigger, and better. To what end do we strive for these things? So that we can one day live a quiet, happy life? So that we can enjoy our family around a table? After squandering our most viable years working ourselves to the bone? After spending years of dinners surrounded by our family while we looked at our phones? So that we can have all the money in the world to do whatever we want, when what we want is already right in front of us?

Consider your own ambitions. What kind of life do you hope for? How does it compare to the life you already have? What are you working toward? What do you imagine life will look like when you've achieved all your goals?

37

Thirty Thousand Feet Up

In the beginning, God created the heavens and the earth.

GENESIS 1:1

. . . .

There's nothing like being thirty thousand feet above the Earth, watching the sun rise over the clouds from an airplane. The sky is every shade of pink and blue, peach and turquoise, and the most incredible shade of orange you'll never find anywhere else.

When I'm viewing the world from this vantage point, I'm always reminded how absolutely tiny we are in the grand scheme of things. From here I can see hundreds of houses, entire lakes, countywide stretches of country roads. I can see clouds for miles and miles. And then I think, *How vast God's love for us must be, if He made all of this and loves every single one of us.*

At home, my view looks different. I see a computer screen, a refrigerator, a bed. I see the "micro" side of life. But we love a micro and macro God. He sees all of it: the expansive landscape and the smallest bud on the tiniest tree. In these moments, when I'm seeing things from the heavens, God reminds me He's got this. He doesn't need me to micromanage. He needs me to function from a place of love, empathy, and forgiveness. And beyond that, He's got the rest. For the God who's literally "got the whole world in His hands," I sure am grateful He loves me too.

Have you experienced the world from a bird's-eye view? What do you know about God when you're up that high and have a different perspective of the world?

Choosing Between Doors

Answer me when I call to you, my righteous God. Give me relief
from my distress; have mercy on me and hear my prayer.

PSALM 4:1 NIV

. . . .

Making decisions can be so scary, can't it? The fear of making the wrong choice keeps me up at night. I tend to play out different scenarios when I should be falling asleep. (I do not recommend this method for resting.) For instance, what if I choose Door 1 and then XYZ terrible thing happens? Or, what if I choose Door 2 and XYZ falls apart? Experts call this *analysis paralysis*. This is when overthinking a decision causes our forward momentum to become paralyzed. Instead of making a choice, we make no choice at all and become stuck in the quicksand of our own thoughts.

In these situations, I've found that taking a decision to God in prayer can be helpful. I don't do this in a fancy way; I just open up to Him. I lay out my fears, my concerns, and what's really on the line with this decision. And when I do that, I usually find a little clarity, and sometimes I feel an inclination toward a certain direction. Do you ever feel that too? I believe this is the Holy Spirit working in us, silently nudging us along the path that's right for us.

Whether you're trying to decide to take the new job opportunity, or make a big move, or even mend a broken friendship, take your decision to God expectantly. He doesn't always lead us to the easiest door to open, but He does help us choose the one He's prepared for us.

Is there a decision you're struggling to make tonight? With an
expectant heart, lay your choices out for God in prayer.

A Few Still Moments

"Come to Me, all you who are weary and burdened, and I will give you rest."

MATTHEW 11:28 NASB

. . . .

Tonight, I have a prayer that may seem a little out of the ordinary:

> *I pray that you have a few minutes of ordinary—of plain old being. I hope you have some precious moments where the inbox doesn't ding, the phone doesn't beep, and the doorbell doesn't ring. A few moments of stillness, sitting, and observing. I pray you're soothed by the rhythm of your breath, the sound of the fan, the sweet scents of a place that brings you peace.*

> *I pray that your moments of stillness remind you the world will keep spinning if you sit for a while. The work will be there, waiting to be picked back up when you are ready. But just for a few minutes, I pray you put down the to-do list, the unfinished project, the insatiable need to be productive.*

So often, we thrive on control. So often, we feel better when we're productive and moving things forward. But I don't think we were meant to go this fast that often. I think sometimes God wants us to sit and breathe and *be*. I don't know exactly what He wants us to learn from this. I'm still learning too. So I'll keep sitting here, praying my prayer for the moments of stillness.

> *Take a few minutes to sit and observe. Listen to the sounds, breathe in the smells, and feel the textures of wherever you are. Feel a soft blanket. Sip a calming tea. Take a deep breath.*

40

Reflection

It's not often we allow ourselves the chance to step back and take a good look at the trajectory our lives are on—to evaluate our path and the choices we've made that have brought us to where we are today. If you're feeling stuck or unsure about where you're headed, borrow this prayer:

Lord, I lay it all at Your feet—every last ounce of my doubt, my fear, and my worry. I trust You. I do. I trust You with my whole life. Be near me, Lord, as I walk this road. Be the voice I hear when I make the next decision. Be the hand I hold when I turn the next corner. Stay by my side until the way forward is clear.

Share your heart with God here:

_____

_____

_____

_____

_____

_____

_____

_____

_____

Rest in the love of a God who adores you.

WEEK

06

A Nest, Not a Bubble

He said, "Come." So Peter got out of the boat and
walked on the water and came to Jesus.

MATTHEW 14:29

As a mom, there are these moments when you look at your children and real-ize they're not little kids anymore. They're growing. They're trying new things and winning and losing. I'll never forget my then-five-year-old twins, Tyler and Caroline, during their first track meet. (Wow, was Caroline fast and Tyler determined!) That same week, my older son, Brady, had spent three nights camping with his dad. They'd been fly-fishing, zip-lining, and horseback riding. Brady called to tell me about it a few days into the trip, and I swear I'd never heard him sound more alive in his ten-and-a-half years.

For Bryan and me, our hopes and dreams for our kids mean that our home is the nest, not the bubble. We're the safe place to come back to after they do the things, try the things, and step out on their own.

I believe God wants us to explore the world He has created for us—to taste and see all that is good. I also believe He wants us to return home when it's time to rest. Flying away to learn and grow. Returning home to rest and reflect. A rhythm of growth.

What role do adventure and discovery play in your life? How are you opening your eyes to new worlds? Is there a skill you've wanted to learn or a place you've dreamed of visiting? Grab your journal and write a list of adventures you'd love to take.

DAY 27

Sunrises, Songs, and Sleepy Hands

Let all that I am praise the LORD; may I never
forget the good things he does for me.

PSALM 103:2 NLT

It was 7:00 a.m. on a Wednesday. Bryan was out of town for work, and Brady was at a sleepaway camp with our church. Tyler and Caroline asked to sleep in my room in their sleeping bags—to have a true "campout." I obliged. As the sun began to peek through the curtains, I opened my eyes to see two sleepy little blue eyes looking back at me.

"Hi, Mommy," Caroline said.

"Hi, sweet girl," I replied. She looked at me and, with a somewhat puzzled look on her face, picked up her hand and placed it on my face. "My hand's asleep. Feel it?" She pressed her hand on my cheek, clearly certain that I could feel the pin pricks that come when you've slept on your arm for too long.

"Oh, dear!" I said, playing along. I scooped her up and planted little kisses all over her face. *What joy,* I thought. *The sun, the warm bed, this precious little girl and her silly six-year-old thoughts.*

Sometimes God speaks to us through sunrises, songs, sleepy faces, and sleepy hands. He delights in us when we delight in Him.

Think about the small joys you noticed throughout your day.
Tomorrow, when you notice these joys again, say aloud, "I hear you,
Lord. Thank You."

Dragons and Good Guys

Like cold water to a thirsty soul, so is good news from a far country.

PROVERBS 25:25

Come away with me, my love. Let's leave behind the worries and aches of today and tomorrow and escape to a place where kings and queens reign, where dragons are slayed, where interesting creatures tell tales.

Come away with me, my child. Let's shut the headlines of the world outside and curl up here on this couch. I'll read a page, and you read a page. Together, we'll learn of myths and secrets, fables and tragedies, lessons and victories.

Come away with me, my heart. Dim the lights and draw up a blanket. You weren't made for this world. That is why it disappoints you. There is magic between the first page and last. The princess finds her prince. The sleeping beauty wakes. The world is always set right side up again.

Turn the pages with me, my love, and savor the rich words, the other worlds, the winding, wonderful stories. Here, good triumphs over evil. True love conquers all. And friendship never falters. Every weird and wonderful creature has a home here. And the good guy always wins.

Find a good book. Maybe a fairy tale or a beloved piece of literature. Solo, or with a child, spend some time in another world, another story.

Tremendous Love

We love because he first loved us.

1 JOHN 4:19

. . . .

One day, when Brady was in fifth grade, Bryan and I went to a parent-teacher conference. But this wasn't just any conference—this one was student-led. Brady would be leading his two teachers, Bryan, and me through a conversation about his progress, growth, goals, and future ambitions. Over the course of twenty-five minutes, Brady reflected on his quizzes and tests, noting where he could have improved and what he was proud of. He told us his goals for the next quarter and how he'd be working toward them.

I hung on to every word, but at some point, it was like I was removed from myself, looking down on what was unfolding. Here sat my firstborn, heart of my heart, leading a conference with conviction, confidence, and humility. My heart overflowed.

It's amazing to think that God reveres us in the same way—with so much pride for who we are and who we are becoming, despite our shortcomings, our mistakes, or our test scores.

 Consider one person in your life you love tremendously. Now consider the fact that God loves you even more than you could ever love that person who has your heart. As you lie down this evening, remember you are treasured, beloved, and worthy.

47

A Place to Rest

Blessed be the God and Father of our Lord Jesus Christ, the Father of mercies and God of all comfort, who comforts us in all our affliction so that we may be able to comfort those who are in any affliction with the comfort with which we ourselves are comforted by God.

2 CORINTHIANS 1:3–4 NASB

Little one, you came into my room last night four times. *Four.* First, it was the noises outside. Second, it was the glass of water you needed. And after the fourth time I saw you clutching your tattered monkey, eyes wide awake and full of hope for Mama to make it all better—whatever *it* was—I realized no glass of water or extra tuck-in would cut it.

I scooted over and pulled you into my warm covers. You didn't say a word, just curled into me and let me brush your hair with my fingertips. After a while your breathing slowed, and I felt your belly taking big breaths. All was calm; all was right. Your daddy scooped you up and carried you to your bedroom.

I don't know what was on your mind, but you needed someone to love you, to remind you that you were seen, that you had a safe place to be. Sometimes I don't know what's making *my* heart feel uneasy either. Sometimes sleep feels far away for me too. And in those moments, having a soft place to land matters a whole lot.

 When you feel uneasy or weary, rest in the love of a God who adores you, who will always make space for you. Spend a few minutes listening to your breath and finding comfort in His arms as you calm your body for sleep.

Reflection

I've been a mother for nearly twelve years now. But before a baby was ever laid in my arms, I knew there was a mother's love inside me.

Maybe you feel that too? Real, whole, unbridled love. These moments of unabashed love are the best parts of life. They're the stuff of memories we'll take with us to heaven. If we're not careful, though, we'll miss them. They'll pass us by like traffic on the freeway, a hurried conversation, or a quick kiss goodnight.

Over the next few pages, reflect on the moments of true love that have made up your life so far.

A moment when someone needed me:

_____

_____

_____

_____

_____

_____

_____

_____

_____

_____

A memory of true love given and received in return:

_____

_____

_____

_____

_____

_____

_____

_____

The truest form of love I know:

_____

_____

_____

_____

_____

_____

_____

_____

This is what love means to me:

_____

_____

_____

_____

_____

_____

_____

_____

_____

_____

_____

_____

_____

_____

_____

_____

_____

_____

_____

_____

Give yourself
the grace to
truly live life
as it happens.

WEEK

07

Happy Place

For the earth will be filled with the knowledge of the
glory of the LORD as the waters cover the sea.

HABAKKUK 2:14

Our family has a happy place. A place that soothes our souls and makes us feel just a little more at home. Perhaps you do too? In May, the Florida beaches are typically wide open, beckoning all the beachgoers with clear turquoise water and beautiful, comfortable, not-quite-the-devil's-attic temperatures. And so off we go, parchment-wrapped ham-and-cheese sandwiches in hand (sliced diagonally, of course), bottles of water for all, and more sunscreen than any one family needs.

Over the next few hours, we chase crabs, pretend to surf, and play in the sand. Every time I'm here, I spend a few minutes staring at the endless waters of the Gulf. It speaks to the vastness of God's creation and His boundless love for us.

Where is *your* happy place? Is it a cabin in the mountains? Or that spot on the shore you visited as a child? Maybe your happy place is at your mom's kitchen table, a cup of tea in front of you. Wherever it is, let your heart go there for a minute today. Remember the colors, the sounds, the smells. Take some time away while you remember why that place fills you up.

Tonight, why don't you borrow this prayer?

Lord, thank You for the feeling of home. Thank You for my happy place. Please be with me as I find a happy place in Your presence. Refresh my heart and mind, and help me keep my eyes pointed toward what matters most. Amen.

54

Nacho Day

He will yet fill your mouth with laughter, and your lips with shouting.

JOB 8:21

. . . .

I have a friend who makes nachos when someone in her family has a tough day. I was a little confused by this at first. I assumed it was just a random tradition. When I think of comfort food, I think meat loaf, chicken soup, or my mom's chicken-and-rice casserole. So I asked her about it: "Why not chicken noodle soup?"

"Because," she said, "soup doesn't make anyone laugh."

"Huh?" I asked, trying to figure out what's funny about chips and cheese.

"Listen," she explained, "when my daughter has a bad day at school, when someone says something unkind or she performs poorly on a test she studied really hard for, I tell her that sometimes it's just nacho day."

Still confused, I blinked.

She put her hand on her forehead. "Nacho. *Not yo.* It's *not yo day.* Nacho Day."

Finally, I got it—and *I love it.*

Sometimes, our bad days lead to correction or untangling big feelings or a good cry on the couch. And sometimes our bad days just need a little levity. A lot changes when we have someone in our lives who can make us laugh and feed us well.

 Some days are great days. Some days are nacho days. How do you bounce back from a day that just plain doesn't go your way?

55

Standard of Grace

He has told you, O man, what is good; and what does the LORD require of you but to do justice, and to love kindness, and to walk humbly with your God?

MICAH 6:8

Does God care about how pretty your pantry is? No. Does God check in on our messy closets? Probably not. But does God find value in peace and order? Yes. We know this from 1 Corinthians 14:40: "Everything should be done in a fitting and orderly way" (NIV).

I find it very interesting that this concept of order and rhythm is spiritually valuable, and yet perfection isn't the point. By placing value on managing our minutes well and on stewarding our resources in a selfless and giving way, we honor God's call to us to do justice, love kindness, and walk humbly with Him. When we plan and organize our calendars, we are able to make time for friends, for caring for others, and for worshiping. When we keep our homes somewhat neat and tidy, we're able to comfortably host others, to function well as a family, and to rest.

God does not call us to be perfect in these areas. Instead, I think God wants us to keep our hearts and our eyes trained on what's important. Perfection was achieved only by Jesus, and it's not expected of you. So you can lay down your standard and embrace what matters most.

In what areas have you been holding yourself to a standard of perfection? Your home? Your work? Your parenting? Your food choices or to-do list? Whatever it is, I invite you to lay down your perfection and embrace a standard of grace so you can focus on what's most important.

A Quick Declutter

My God will supply every need of yours according
to his riches in glory in Christ Jesus.

PHILIPPIANS 4:19

Okay, friend, we're going to get tactical tonight. Because sometimes we need a dose of inspiration, and sometimes we just need a kick in the pants, *amiright*? Just give me ten minutes, and I promise you're going to sleep better.

Physical clutter is mental clutter. And what better way to wind down for the evening than by clearing the clutter in both spaces. Now, don't be scared off by this interruption in our regular devotions. I want you to take ten minutes to clear the clutter wherever you can. Just ten, no longer.

You may have overstuffed closets or junk drawers that could use your attention someday. But we're not talking about that tonight. We're talking about the high-traffic areas that could use some love so that your life runs more smoothly.

Think about one of the places in your home that your family uses most. Can you take a few things off your kitchen counters? Could you recycle the shampoo bottles with only a *little* shampoo you've been keeping under the bathroom sink? Remember, how we spend our moments is how we spend our lives. If you spend ten minutes of your day cursing all the junk on your countertops, you could flip those minutes into moments of peace as you add some calm to the chaos. Future-you will thank current-you for caring for her so well.

Consider how you might incorporate a few short minutes of cleanup into your daily evening routine. How might this practice improve your peace of mind?

Throwaway Days

"My grace is sufficient for you, for my power is made perfect in weakness."

2 CORINTHIANS 12:9

. . . .

This one's for the girl who had to throw her plans out the window today. Who has the sick baby, the aging parent, the washing machine that overflowed . . . again. Who feels defeated, like you might not ever catch up.

Here's what I want you to know: It's okay that you had to set aside the things you'd hoped to conquer today. It's okay to show up for your life and do what you have to do.

These days aren't throwaway days. Oh, no. These are the days when you're doing the *actual* stuff of life. In fact, I'd argue that all that other "stuff" you're conquering is actually in preparation for days like this.

So lean in to the reality of the day that happened to you, and not the day you hoped it would be. Set the panic, the rush, and the to-do list down for the night. Set your email aside, and snuggle your feverish toddler on the couch. Go to bed instead of back to work. Your inbox can wait. Let the dishes sit in the sink and the laundry sit in the hamper, if you need to. Life is messy and unexpected. Give yourself the grace to truly live it as it happens.

How can you show yourself grace tonight? Remember, tomorrow He will make all things new.

Reflection

As much as we'd all love to have it all together all the time, life just doesn't work that way. And yet . . . we still try so hard.

One of the biggest lessons I've learned in my adult life is to choose (and name) what matters most to me. That's where I will invest my time and my effort. I can let the other stuff slide. What's important to me may not be what's important to everyone around me—and that's okay.

And the same goes for you—in your particular season and situation, you may love making beautiful, elaborate meals for your family and not care about throwing elaborate birthday parties. I may love to spend my time gardening while ordering takeout more often than not. Owning your values is incredibly empowering. Make a decision about what's important to you in this season and what's not. Give yourself permission to make decisions that reflect these things.

What's important to me right now:

_____

_____

_____

What's on the back burner at the moment (or, um, forever):

_____

_____

_____

Growth isn't always comfortable. Lean into it.

WEEK

08

· · · · · · · · · · · · · · · · · · · ·

DAY 36

The Altar Call

Jesus said to him, "I am the way, and the truth, and the life.
No one comes to the Father except through me."

JOHN 14:6

As a young adult, I attended a conference in a giant arena with thousands of other believers. On one night, the rule was that upon entering the arena, you had to be completely silent. As my friends and I found our way to our seats, the atmosphere was really moving. Thousands of other people, none speaking, gave silent head nods and smiles. The arena was pitch-black, with only small aisle markers lighting the way. In the center of the arena was a small stage surrounded by hundreds of candles. A popular Christian band walked onto the stage to perform an acoustic version of a popular worship ballad. I sobbed through the entire song. It felt like God was in every ounce of air in that place.

It was so incredibly moving. I crave that emotional faith, that on-stage-type worship, that big-event-type closeness to God. But as a thirty-something mom to three kids, I don't have those experiences often.

Instead, I'm learning to become comfortable with a liturgical practice of faith. Instead of hands high in the air singing my praises to God, I offer up thanks while making the third ham-and-cheese sandwich. I find that He meets me when my patience runs low during bedtime routines. This everyday, ordinary, repetitive, *Groundhog Day*–type faith isn't groundbreaking or tear-inducing, but it's just as real. And I'm learning to recognize the power in it.

Have you ever had a moving faith experience where you felt your heart swell with joy and worship? What does worship look like to you now? How do you meet with God every day?

Volume Control

One thing I do: forgetting what lies behind and straining
forward to what lies ahead, I press on toward the goal for
the prize of the upward call of God in Christ Jesus.

PHILIPPIANS 3:13–14

· ·

The noise of this world can be so very loud. We flitter from screen to screen, info source to info source. I don't know about you, but I wasn't made to shoulder this much concern, worry, and information all the time. And in our home, we've started turning down the volume on *everything* we own. I've found that once you make an effort to turn down the noise, you'll discover it's coming from all sorts of places way more than you'd imagine.

There are sounds coming from the usual suspects: TV, Spotify playlists, electronic toys, devices. Then there are other bits of visual noise coming from an abundance of stuff: the pile of mail on the counter, the overstuffed drawers, even the over-crammed to-do list. When we turn down that noise, we can discover the harmony of a home and heart that are more peaceful instead.

And if we're going to turn the volume up anywhere, let's do it in places with the best sounds: children's laughter, a favorite song, a conversation with a friend, even the words of an encouraging book. And may we have the wisdom to turn down what distracts us from all that is good. I find that I'm able to hear the voice of God better when I've created a space for Him and unburdened my heart and ears from all the rest.

 Consider the sounds you hear right now. How can you make space for God and for sounds that fill you up?

DAY 38

Pay Attention

And the Spirit of the Lord shall rest upon him, the Spirit of
wisdom and understanding, the Spirit of counsel and might,
the Spirit of knowledge and the fear of the Lord.

ISAIAH 11:2

Do you ever have the feeling that something inside you is shifting? You feel a change happening in your gut, but you're not sure what it means or where it's taking you. It feels like you might be outgrowing your current season. And just like a pair of jeans that doesn't fit quite right, you start to notice yourself bumping up against the edges of the life you're currently living.

This feeling makes me uncomfortable. I love a change of seasons, but only if I'm the one to draw the map and decide where I'm going. When the Holy Spirit moves inside of me, telling me something new is happening, I resist it. Life is just so much easier when I stick to what I'm already good at, even if it no longer fits. At least, that's what I tell myself.

Even though I don't like to admit it, discomfort can be quite useful. The sting of a hot stove tells our brain to remove our hand quickly. The pain of a traumatic experience urges us to seek help. The discomfort of a strained relationship causes us to work to make amends.

Often, the feeling of discomfort is simply inviting us to pay attention. It may be leading us to a new path, or it may be showing us there's another area of our lives we need to focus on. Try to pay attention to that feeling. You may be surprised at what you discover.

 Are you paying attention to your gut right now? What is it telling you about how your life is unfolding?

DAY 39

Eyes on Your Own Paper

Let each one test his own work, and then his reason to boast
will be in himself alone and not in his neighbor.

GALATIANS 6:4

When I was in elementary school, I was a straight-A student. I was a teacher's pet, always-follow-the-rules type of girl. One day, in drama class, we were given a pop quiz. But I didn't know the answers. My choices were to literally turn in my test blank or to copy from the girl next to me. And so, ten-year-old Emily peeked at her neighbor's paper and jotted down her answers.

The guilt I carried consumed me, so I confessed my cheating to the teacher that afternoon. I took a zero for that test and learned a valuable lesson. One that applies not only to tests in elementary school but to life in general.

James Clear, the writer of *Atomic Habits* (one of my favorite books!), compares the adage "eyes on your own paper" to remaining focused on our own lives and callings as adults. It's easy to look around and see others making different choices than we are (like working full-time versus choosing to be a stay-at-home mom, going back to school versus keeping your job) and question the choices we're making. But what's right for one person isn't always right for another. Comparison is the thief of joy. So even if you are staring at a blank page right now, keep your eyes on your own paper. God has called you to this particular season of life. And He's called you to this moment for a very specific purpose.

 Are you looking over at your neighbor's "paper"? Focus your attention on your own path, and rest assured that God has brought you to this calling, this "paper," with love.

65

On Flowers and Weeds

Let your eyes look directly forward, and your gaze be straight before you.

PROVERBS 4:25

. . . .

I went for a walk with my kids the other day. The spring air was not too hot, not too cold—it was just right. As we walked, I thought about who they'd be when they grow up and if I'm doing anything right as a mother and—of course—what in the world we were going to have for dinner that night. Something nourishing but not so green that they wouldn't eat it. Something comforting but not so unhealthy that it would turn them into junk food monsters. And then . . .

My son ran for a weed. My immediate thought was to tell him to put it down; it's a weed, for goodness' sake. But it was a *purple* weed, and so it had to be picked. It was then that I realized he had handfuls of weeds. Yellow ones. Pink ones. White ones.

"They're for you, Mom!" he shouted, adding the last bloom to the bunch. I smiled, took a deep breath, and received my treasures. My, what we miss when we're distracted.

When was the last time you gave yourself time to look up? To see what's right in front of you instead of being consumed with what's in your head? Try it right now. Write down one thing you're grateful for.

Reflection

What are you learning right now? If you're unsure, think of the ways you're feeling stretched. Perhaps with a project at work or a relationship or a difficult parenting situation. Growth isn't always comfortable. Lean into those parts of life that feel a little challenging right now.

What are you learning lately?

_____

_____

What do you hope to learn in the days ahead?

_____

_____

How is this growth shaping you into who you want to become?

_____

_____

_____

What steps can you take to help facilitate this growth?

_____

_____

_____

_____

God is
teaching me
to get comfortable
with the doing,
not just the
done.

WEEK

09

. . . .

Perfection

For all have sinned and fall short of the glory of God.

ROMANS 3:23

. . . .

When my oldest son was born, the first few weeks went by in a blur. Between learning how to breastfeed, managing mountains of laundry, and coping with sleep deprivation (that precious child never wanted to sleep), I was barely getting by. But once the postpartum fog wore off and we regained a little semblance of normalcy (read: he started sleeping consistently through the night), I set out to prove that I could be a work-from-home mother and wife who accomplished great things, kept her house neat and tidy, had dinner on the table every night at six o'clock, and raised a perfectly well-behaved child.

I'm sure you can see where this is going.

I had created this standard in my head of what "a good wife and mom" looked like. Quite literally, from what her appearance looked like to how her child behaved to how she navigated her life. "She" was perfect. I, however, was real.

My attempts to attain this level of perfection kept me from living the life God was calling me to live. He didn't create that standard for me (in fact, He didn't expect me to be perfect in all those ways *at all*). Instead, I'd allowed social media, the outside world, and my own fantasies to hold me to a standard that was impossible to reach. It was only when I realized that *no one* was expecting perfection from me that I was able to loosen up, to get comfortable with mess, and to find joy in the journey.

Where in your life are you expecting yourself to reach a standard of perfection? What would it look like to be good and joyful in that area, rather than perfect?

70

The Doing

I can do all things through Christ who strengthens me.

PHILIPPIANS 4:13 NKJV

As a writer, I love the feeling of holding a finished book in my hands. But the process of writing is sometimes quite painful. I question myself and my abilities, stare out the window, find anything to do to procrastinate what needs to be done.

But God is teaching me to get comfortable with the *doing*, not just the *done*. Finished products are easy to celebrate. We reflect on our hard work, and we have something (hopefully) wonderful to show for it.

But the doing . . . that's another story. God is teaching me to be excellent at the process and to enjoy it along the way. God doesn't want me to only celebrate having accomplished things, but to celebrate the forward momentum.

What's the art or skill He's calling you to practice? Perhaps you're a teacher. A graduating class is fantastic, but the hours you spent instructing your students—that is your art, your work, your daily practice.

Are you a nurse? Having a patient fully healed is worthy of a party. But the act of replacing bandages and tending to those who are ill—that is your art. That is your skill honed through thousands of hours of practice at work.

Are you a mother? Celebrating milestones is fantastic, but celebrating the work of mothering is where true discipleship happens. The patient words, the books read. This is the art of living into your calling, day after day.

What is your work? Your art? How can you celebrate the process of doing as much as you celebrate the end result?

DAY 43

Progress, Not Perfection

Therefore, if anyone is in Christ, he is a new creation. The
old has passed away; behold, the new has come.

2 CORINTHIANS 5:17

Have you ever set out to make a change, only to fall short and have to begin again? Day Ones are so hard. The beginning of a new project, the start of a new workout plan, or the day you decided to end the addiction.

Recently, I worked with a nutritionist to learn how certain foods affected me and to develop better eating habits to help fuel my body for all that life requires of it. I did great for a few weeks, then off the wagon I fell. (Sometimes, it's just so hard to say no to nachos.) I threw caution to the wind for a while, until my body started reminding me how terrible it feels when I'm consistently making poor choices.

And so here I am, and my Day One begins again. After all, it's progress I'm after, not perfection. A year from now, I'll be glad I got back on the wagon. If you're staring at Day One, too, I feel you. So begin something today that future-you will be grateful for. Because it's never too late to begin again.

What do you need to begin again? Will tomorrow be your next Day One? Don't forget: God has made you strong and courageous. And He'll give you strength so you won't grow weary in doing the good work you've been called to do.

72

The Weight of Perfection

Therefore, since we are surrounded by so great a cloud of witnesses,
let us also lay aside every weight, and sin which clings so closely,
and let us run with endurance the race that is set before us.

HEBREWS 12:1

Hi, my name is Emily, and I am a struggling perfectionist.

Even as I write those words, I squirm a little because I am still *very much* battling my perfectionist tendencies. I'd like for my home to be spotless, my inbox to be sorted, and my children to be wonderfully behaved at all times, pretty please. Also, I would like to have abundant energy, flawless skin, and wear the jeans I wore in college. Thank you.

And yet, while I'm able to achieve some of those things some of the time (minus the jeans from college), I'm never able to achieve all of them at the same time. And even when I'm able to achieve one of them, I've sometimes realized that perfection wasn't worth the cost.

In those moments I often ask myself, *Can I choose good instead of perfect?*

Good is a lived-in home. A space with storage and systems, baskets for blankets, boxes for toys, and a junk drawer for quickly cleaning off the kitchen counter. Our home isn't perfect at all times, but it's lived in. It's full of love. It's flexible and messy and real. And that is so much better than perfect.

I carried the weight of perfectionism for a long time. It is a heavy
weight to carry and an unachievable, unmaintainable standard to
aspire to. What weight are you carrying right now? What would your
life look like if you laid that weight aside?

73

I Am Healing

Heal me, O Lord, and I shall be healed; save me, and
I shall be saved, for you are my praise.

JEREMIAH 17:14

. . . .

I once met with a therapist during a particularly busy season. I was managing a lot of things at work and at home, and I was struggling to stop "over-functioning" and burning myself out. My therapist and I talked about perfectionism and my tendency to go all-in, all the time—and how God's grace saves us from having to reach for such a lofty goal.

A few months into our work together, I remember telling her, "I love my kids. I love my job. I love my husband. I want to be good at all my jobs, but I am trying so hard not to be that stressed-out, frazzled, overwhelmed-all-the-time woman I once was."

"You are healing," she said to me. "Recite these words to yourself whenever you feel those feelings coming to the surface: *I am healing.*"

Whether you are healing from perfectionism, burnout, over-functioning, trauma, illness, or grief, place your hand on your heart whenever you need to. Remind yourself, "I am healing." Allow God's grace to wash over you again and again throughout the day. Allow it to release you from the bonds of perfectionism and usher you into a new way forward.

Reflection

Perfectionism can steal a whole lot of joy from your life. But loosening our grip often leaves us feeling out of control. When you're feeling overwhelmed, you can borrow this prayer or write your own:

Lord, take the reins from me. I feel like I have to do everything wonderfully, perfectly, all by myself. But I know that's not true. When I become fixated on perfection, show me the goodness in the mess. When I become hyper-focused on productivity, remind me of the importance of slowing down. Help me notice and accept Your grace in my life as I go about my day.

May the
Lord meet you
right where
you are.

WEEK

10

· · · · · · · · · · · · · · · · · ·

On Grief

Count it all joy, my brothers, when you meet trials of various kinds.

JAMES 1:2

. . . .

Grief is a funny thing. It comes and goes, washing over us at random and often inopportune times. Sometimes sadness finds us when a song on the radio nudges us just right. Or when we turn the page of the calendar to see *that* date. Or when the smell of the Christmas tree reminds you of her frail, precious hand in yours.

Sometimes grief shows up as tears that fall without warning. Sometimes it feels more like a weighted blanket, a constant heaviness. Recently, a friend told me that grief is simply love with no place to go. And that explanation made a lot of sense to me. If that is true, then grief, in and of itself, is somewhat of a beautiful thing. May we count it pure joy, then, to have had the chance to love someone, even if who we loved is gone.

Still, fixers that we are, we try to do a lot of things with this pain. Numb it. Alleviate it. Ignore it. Stuff it down. But I think this displaced love simply needs the space to be. And so, we move some things around and make a space for it, allowing it to be what it is: beautiful and hard, sometimes big and sometimes small. A special kind of love all its own.

 To make space for grief, we first must name it. If you are grieving, identify the displaced love you're feeling. Instead of trying to alleviate it or push it away, allow it the space to simply be in your heart.

Your Grief Counts

He will wipe away every tear from their eyes, and death shall be no more, neither shall there be mourning, nor crying, nor pain anymore, for the former things have passed away.

REVELATION 21:4

There's grief over the loss of a loved one or the loss of a relationship, but then there's "other" grief. This is sadness over something that doesn't fall into an obvious category of "things to grieve." It's easy to try to talk ourselves out of this sadness, to convince ourselves it doesn't count or isn't worthy of grief.

One day a tiny, hungry kitten showed up on my back porch. I'd never owned a cat because my boys are allergic, and I'd generally considered myself "not a cat person." But over the course of three days, this little girl curled right up into my lap and made a space in my heart. She sat next to my computer while I worked. She followed me around the house. She settled into my lap whenever I sat down. And when I handed her to the kind family who adopted her, my heart broke a little.

I loved this sweet girl. I loved the way she made me slow down and feel present in the moment. I loved her little nose and her raspy meows. My love for her had no place to go when she left. Though I considered my grief over a cat I'd owned for three days somewhat silly, I gave my feelings space to sort themselves, to exist, and to be. To have loved her for just a few days was a joy.

 Is there a sadness you've buried? A grief you previously decided didn't count? Honor the authenticity of your feelings by allowing them the space to exist without judgement.

79

Don't Trudge Alone

O Lord, all my longing is before you; my sighing is not hidden from you.
PSALM 38:9 ESV

. . . .

What I know about Jesus is this: He isn't done with you yet. You are not too old, too broken, or too far gone. He pursues us. And He hasn't forgotten you.

What might feel like melancholy, languishing, or trudging through thick mud in unwieldy rubber boots may actually be Jesus pulling on you. *Notice Me. Listen to Me. Stop a minute for Me.*

But as humans, we struggle greatly with slowing down. Our culture tells us we're only growing if we're moving forward. I wonder, though, if we could also grow by stopping. Standing still in the thick mud, pausing the day-to-day, or sitting in our pile of tasks and laundry and feelings for a minute.

Maybe then, if we turned down the volume on our momentum or our trudging, we'd hear Him. If we made a space for Him, He'd come and sit next to us. "You're doing okay, sweet girl," He'd say. "You're doing the hard and repetitive stuff of life. Do not grow weary. I am here to help you. You don't have to trudge alone."

Discovering God's mercies and delights in the mundane requires patience, focus, and intention. As you go about your day, keep your heart open to His whisperings and gifts.

Take His Hand

He reached down from on high and took hold of
me; he drew me out of deep waters.

PSALM 18:16 NIV

. . . .

I was tired and thirsty, and You were there. Even though I'd failed again and again and again, You still met me in my weakness. I didn't deserve You to reach out Your hand and help me up. I didn't deserve You to turn Your face toward me when so many others who were living with more wisdom and courage deserved your attention. And yet, You came to me.

It wasn't the first time You'd extended a hand to help me up. In fact, a few times in the past, You'd reached for me, and I'd swatted You away. "I don't need You. I've got this," I'd say. And with a gentle smile and a soft hand, You'd reach out to me. Again and again.

This time, I haven't just fallen . . . I'm broken. The ache in me is so deep. I'm too mangled, too tangled, too much of a mess. A lost cause. A hopeless case. A girl too far gone. Lost in worry, drowning in what-ifs, and tired. Oh, so tired.

You never tire of getting down on Your knee, reaching toward me, and helping me up. You are not impatient with me. You are not angry, though I'd understand if You were. You are gentle and kind and loving. You see the tiny flame flickering inside me and believe in me when I no longer believe in myself. It's because of You that I will stand up again.

If you've fallen into old habits or worry-spirals again, God is not done with you. Look up. Look for His hand. He hasn't forgotten you. He will always show up.

Check-In

Let us hold tightly without wavering to the hope we affirm,
for God can be trusted to keep his promise.

HEBREWS 10:23 NLT

. . . .

Welcome to the halfway point! It's been an amazing fifty days discovering God's peace and rest with you. Tonight, I invite you to reflect on how things have changed and the ways in which you've grown over the last fifty days. Consider the following questions.

- How is God working in your life? What challenges has He placed in front of you to help you grow?
- What moments, over the last few weeks, are you proud of?
- What difficulties do you find yourself facing repeatedly? How might you work to alleviate those pain points?
- Is God calling you into a new season right now? Or encouraging you to find peace in your current situation?
- What hopes do you have for the next fifty days? Is there a skill you'd like to improve or a goal you'd like to achieve? Present your hopes to God in prayer and invite Him to walk alongside you on this next journey.

 A prayer for you:
May the Lord meet you right where you are. May He plant within you
a bold spirit of hope and faith in what's to come. May you trust that He
is the King of all kings, the Creator of all things, our Miracle Worker.
(PS: Next time you're in the shower, turn on the song "Oceans" by
Hillsong UNITED. Sing it loudly.)

WEEK 10

Reflection

Here we are, halfway through this journey of discovering and celebrating God's nearness and faithfulness. Tonight, let's spend some time evaluating exactly where you are right now.

How are you, truly?

_____

_____

_____

_____

_____

_____

_____

_____

_____

_____

_____

_____

What has changed for you over the last ten weeks?

_____

_____

_____

_____

_____

_____

_____

_____

_____

Now that you are more aware of God moving in your life, what small moments have you noticed in His presence?

_____

_____

_____

_____

_____

_____

_____

_____

What is troubling you right now?

_____

_____

_____

_____

_____

_____

_____

What brought you joy today?

_____

_____

_____

_____

_____

_____

_____

_____

_____

_____

You are loved.
God is for you.
He keeps His word.

WEEK

11

The Real Fruit of Summer

But the fruit of the Spirit is love, joy, peace, patience, kindness, goodness, faithfulness, gentleness, self-control; against such things there is no law.

GALATIANS 5:22–23

Where we live in Pensacola, summertime is such a beautiful season. The Gulf of Mexico is the brightest shade of turquoise. The white sand is so lovely and inviting. Our days are filled with trips to the beach, picnics outside, and road trips to visit friends and family. It's a wonderful few months.

But sometimes, summertime is stressful. Children are out of school. Schedules and structures are looser. The kids eat twelve Popsicles a day and stay up way too late as the day stretches longer into the evening. Family life and attitudes can get a bit hairy. If I'm not careful, things can spiral in the wrong direction. And not just with them, but with *me*.

Whether you naturally thrive on structured routine, or if a more relaxed pace is more your speed, ask God to fill you with His Spirit. Because when we gather the fruit of the Holy Spirit—every ounce of love, joy, peace, patience, kindness, goodness, faithfulness, gentleness, and self-control we have—we can navigate this more relaxed, fun-filled season in a different way. We can offer our children the best versions of ourselves by mirroring Jesus to them.

How can you approach a conversation or an act of service with the fruit of the Spirit gathered in your arms? Which one do you struggle with the most? Ask Him to help you "cultivate" that fruit in your life.

Your Joy Is My Joy

But grow in the grace and knowledge of our Lord and Savior Jesus Christ. To him be the glory both now and to the day of eternity. Amen.

2 PETER 3:18

My daughter, Caroline, walked out of school to the car pickup line holding the hand of her teacher and the hand of her best friend, who is *my* best friend's daughter. Caroline was going to her first sleepover, and she was ecstatic. I watched her climb into my best friend's car as I sat in mine, two cars behind, since I was picking up her brother Tyler. Excitement radiated from her smile and from the bounce in her step. Because Caroline is young, I'm typically right in the middle of her joy since I've probably facilitated it myself. But on this day, I witnessed her joy not from the stage where it was taking place, but from the second row. An onlooker, not a participant.

I waved at her with a smile, wanting to be part of this happy moment. As I placed my hand in my lap, I thought to myself, *I waved and you didn't see me, but that's okay. Enjoy your joy, sweet girl.* I don't know where the thought came from; it was almost as if God spoke the words to me Himself.

Watching our children spread their wings is a tender and wonderful thing. It creates both an ache and a smile in my heart. Sometimes I wonder if God sees us this way, too, as His own children. Our lives are unfolding, and He is waving with an ache and a smile, hoping we will look over to Him.

If you have a child you love, how has it felt to tenderly watch his or her life unfold? Consider God, our Father, witnessing your growth the same way. Give thanks to the One who made a way for you.

89

Unpacking

*Lead me in your truth and teach me, for you are the God
of my salvation; for you I wait all the day long.*

PSALM 25:5

My little boy's nightly routine is to search his room for his beloved stuffed monkey before bed. During bath time and stories, he talks about everything from recess games to his disdain for tomatoes to the new LEGO magazine. But as his head hits the pillow and I join him for prayers, he quietly says, "Mom, will you be in heaven when I'm there?"

The sudden shift in topics startles me but doesn't surprise me. I recognize this rhythm. Big thoughts and questions tend to surface when my children slow their little bodies and minds at night. I treasure those few moments and the opportunity to speak truth to my kids, to remind them they are safe and loved before they close their eyes.

I gently lean in and tell him we'll all be together in heaven one day. We thank Jesus together for His promises and His love for us, and my little boy drifts off to sleep. Watching his chest rise and fall, I'm reminded how important it is for me to stick around a few extra moments at bedtime. How natural it is for hearts of all ages to unpack big thoughts and worries when the day begins to slow down. And how important it is to be reminded of what's true about ourselves and of the world.

You are loved. God is for you. He keeps His word.

What truth about God do you need to remember? Write it down. You might even write it on a Post-it note and put it somewhere visible so that you'll be reminded each evening before you go to bed.

'Tis But a Season

For everything there is a season, and a time for every matter under heaven.

ECCLESIASTES 3:1

. . . .

Every morning, I walk outside to see the sun rise. I've tried to take a photo of this incredibly beautiful event so many times. But never does a photo ever capture the magnificence of it. Grounding myself in this rhythm every morning helps me remember the cyclical nature of our lives. Sun up, sun down. Winter comes, winter goes. Breathe in, breathe out.

Little boys with skinny legs and untied shoes will one day grow up to become men. The blazing heat of August will eventually give way to the breezes of September. The seasons of sleepless nights and hard work will one day yield to a slower pace.

If you are in a challenging season, take heart. Winter will eventually turn to spring. The bare branches will begin to bear little green leaves. The sun will peak from behind the clouds. Stay the course.

What season are you in today? Is it one to savor? Perhaps it's one to simply get through? Make your season known to God, and ask for His guidance while you journey through.

Midnight Oil

She sees that her trading is profitable, and her lamp does not go out at night.

PROVERBS 31:18 NIV

To you, the mother gathering energy you didn't know you had for one more feeding, one more diaper change, one more lullaby. You are loved. The love you are giving matters.

To you, the entrepreneur with the big idea, trying and trying again, then starting over and trying again. Squeezing in every minute you can before your "real job" calls with the sound of your alarm. You are loved. The work you are doing matters.

To you, the writer, questioning her skills by the light of a candle, filling pages with words, only to delete them all and begin again. Riding the waves of joy and despair that make up the chase of a dream. You are loved. The words you are writing matter.

And to you, the keeper of the home. The one who's tucked little ones into bed, kissed little heads, and quietly shut bedroom doors. Whose own rest will only come once the dishes and the laundry and the tidying up from the day are done. You are loved. The endless tasks you complete in love matter.

 Some seasons of life require us to burn the midnight oil, to work when others rest. Remember, your trading is profitable. Stay the course and remember, this is but for a season.

Reflection

Have you ever spent a season wishing for the next one to arrive (for the graduation, the engagement, the wedding, the child, the job), only to find yourself reminiscing about the season once it had passed? We all do it. But what if we found the joy in the middle of the season we're in *while we're in it*? Let this be an experiment in noticing the goodness around you.

_____

_____

_____

_____

_____

_____

_____

_____

_____

_____

_____

_____

_____

_____

When you find
a true friend,
hold onto her.

WEEK

12

. . . .

The Truest of Friends

A friend loves at all times, and a brother is born for a time of adversity.

PROVERBS 17:17 NIV

Find a true friend, a real one. When you find her, hold onto her. Keep her, love her, thank her. Remember her birthday, her children's birthdays, the day her grandmother passed into the arms of Jesus. Put the dates on your calendar. Pray for her on the day of her mammogram. Take her supper when the hard stuff collides. Give her space when she needs to withdraw, and hold onto her when she is coming undone.

Be the real one for her hard days. See past her "I'm fine, really" and into her "Please come over with a bag of M&Ms." Remind her she is good at her life. And tell her the truth when she asks for your thoughts.

To have one true friend in this life is to have a treasure. Hold onto her.

Do you have a real, true friend? Who is she? If not, what friend might you reach out to today to show some love and forge a stronger bond?

96

Lake Life

How many are your works, LORD! In wisdom you made
them all; the earth is full of your creatures.

PSALM 104:24 NIV

During the summer, when the days are long and the air is warm, our family loves to travel to our favorite lake in Georgia. It's our happy place, and escaping to the lake is one of our most anticipated family traditions.

For us, lake life symbolizes a return to slow living. We take long walks through the woods, stay up late to make s'mores by the campfire, and find that we live outside more than we live inside. At the lake, there aren't a lot of big buildings, so the night sky is a sight to behold. It's a rich shade of black, dotted by more stars than I can see when we're back home in the city.

It's here in the wilderness, surrounded by God's creation and my favorite people, that I feel so connected to Him. I feel like His creativity—in the landscape, in the lake, and in the unique people He's placed in my life—is on full display. Leaving the lake is always like leaving a little piece of my heart. But I take the memories with me, tuck them in my pocket, and am renewed with a sense of gratitude for slowing down and savoring the goodness and good people He's filled my life with.

What are your family's traditions? Do you have some that fuel your soul? How do these traditions shape your memories and invite you to be nearer to God?

97

On Pace and Space

"Be still, and know that I am God; I will be exalted among
the nations, I will be exalted in the earth!"

PSALM 46:10 NIV

. . . .

I once read a book called *Breaking Open* during a particularly busy season. (It's phenomenal, by the way. I highly recommend it.) The author, Jacob Armstrong, explores the concepts of pace and space. Keep too quick of a pace, he says, and you'll leave little space for God to be noticed. You won't experience the magic of a meaningful conversation or notice the beauty of the rain as it softly hits the windows or reflect on life right as it happens.

When we move about our days at a frenetic speed, we miss so much. And yet, we often think there's just no other way of doing life. We can't *stop* feeding the baby, we can't *not* cook dinner, we can't *ignore* the laundry forever. And yet . . . I bet we could schedule our must-dos with a little more margin around them. We could put our phone on the charger at 7:00 p.m. so we don't spend the evening distracted. We could take ourselves outside for a ten-minute walk when the overwhelm hits.

We may not have control over everything that's on our plates, but we can set the pace of how we tackle it all. We can ask for a deadline extension. We can delegate responsibilities to our partner. We can ask for help. We can make space.

 What do you need to make space for in your life? Friends?
Community? Time with your partner? Time with God? Remember, you
have more agency over your life than you often realize. Set the pace
and make the space.

Stargazing

He determines the number of the stars; he gives to all of them their names.

PSALM 147:4

. . . .

Have you ever gone out to the country, somewhere the city lights can't reach, where the noise of people and traffic gives way to the quiet hum of the outdoors? Recently, I went away for a weekend with some friends to a cabin deep in the woods of Alabama. Sitting on the dock late one night, we looked up to see thousands, maybe millions, of sparkling stars stretched far over the lake.

I leaned back on my hands for a moment and breathed it all in. The stillness around me stilled something inside me. I knew this wasn't just something you get to see when you're in the middle of the city, or even the suburbs, with streetlights and cars and the hustle of life drowning out this magnificent scene.

We sat for a moment and stared. And then we saw it, a shooting star—so fast we looked at each other to confirm what we'd seen. A bright, white slash across the glittering sky. A God-wink saying, "Welcome. Sit and stay awhile."

Have you ever seen a shooting star? Even if you live in a busy city, sometimes on a clear night you can look up and spot one. They're so quick and beautiful—a reminder of the magic in all God's creation.

99

Living Fully Alive

"The thief comes only to steal and kill and destroy; I have
come that they may have life, and have it to the full."

JOHN 10:10 NIV

. . . .

I write about hard stuff because I often don't know what I feel about a hard thing until I put it to the music of my keyboard. One of my favorite things to do is freewrite, to set a timer for fifteen minutes and give myself the freedom to write just for me. The words come pouring when I open the floodgates and take off the pressure of publication. No one else ever has to read them or know they exist. And when I allow myself to let go, to let my hands fly across the keyboard, I often find that, underneath the pain I'm describing, there's a song. A beautiful song.

If you think about it, pain is similar to love. There's an undercurrent of beauty and passion. Both are feelings we only have when we are truly living with eyes and hearts wide open, awake and aware. When we live this way, we allow ourselves to be fully feeling humans. And that is hard. Because fully feeling humans *feel* everything. Pain and sadness. Joy and excitement. Despair and delight.

Let yourself feel your feelings. It's worth it, even when it's hard.

 Are you showing up to your life as fully present? Or are you burying
the feelings that seem too big or too hard? Have you tried your hand
at journaling? Let the words pour out of you, and see what beautiful
songs come to be.

Reflection

With so many responsibilities, it's hard to slow down. I've been told numerous times I tend to live with my foot on the gas pedal. It's in my nature. I'm driven, ambitious, and fast-paced. But I'm learning that when we operate that way, we miss something. A lot of things, really. It's hard to enjoy the small delights when you're living life with your hair on fire.

As we close out this week, I invite you to spend some time reflecting on the tiny joys of the last few days. Here are a few examples to get your thoughts rolling:

- The feel of a tiny hand in yours as you walk them into school
- A door held open unexpectedly by a kind stranger
- The coziness of a rainy evening at home wearing your comfiest pajamas

What small joys have you noticed this week?

What acts of kindness have you witnessed?

_____

_____

_____

_____

_____

_____

_____

_____

What does slowing down actually feel like to you? Is it
uncomfortable, or does it feel like a relief to take a breather?

_____

_____

_____

_____

_____

_____

_____

_____

Does the idea of slowing down spark any fear in you? If so, why?

_____

_____

_____

_____

_____

_____

_____

_____

What good could come from a slower pace of life?

_____

_____

_____

_____

_____

_____

_____

_____

What is the next right thing for you?

WEEK

13

. . . .

Now I Lay Me Down to Sleep

*I will say to the L*ORD*, "My refuge and my fortress, my God, in whom I trust."*

PSALM 91:2

I love learning about liturgy. For anyone unfamiliar with it (as I was not long ago), *liturgy* is a public ritual of worship. In my head, though maybe not on paper, it means "scripted." The parts of the service at our new church follow a certain order, and the prayers we recite together are drawn from *The Book of Common Prayer*. I recently came across this prayer and wanted to share it with you today:

> *Keep watch, dear Lord, with those who work, or watch, or weep this night, and give your angels charge over those who sleep. Tend the sick, Lord Christ; give rest to the weary, bless the dying, soothe the suffering, pity the afflicted, shield the joyous; and all for your love's sake. Amen.*

This prayer was written by St. Augustine of Hippo around the fifth century AD. It's so beautiful to think that people have been praying these same words for over fifteen hundred years. I hope they bring you comfort today.

 Is there a prayer that is meaningful to you? Here is a favorite from when I was a child:
Now I lay me down to sleep, I pray the Lord my soul to keep. If I shall live another day, I pray the Lord will show me the way.

Rinse and Repeat

Therefore, my beloved brothers, be steadfast, immovable, always abounding in the work of the Lord, knowing that in the Lord your labor is not in vain.

1 CORINTHIANS 15:58

When a hurricane hits, I know exactly what to do. Sand bags. Water jugs. Flashlights. Instant coffee. When a friend goes through a crisis, I'm ready. Casseroles. Meal trains. Prayers. Those peak moments in life—the crisis, the holiday, the performance, the big game—I know how to handle those.

It's the in-between that gets me. Teaching how to tie shoes. Again. Searching for said shoes. Again. Making dinner, doing homework . . . again. The moments that lie in between the moments of high stress, high drama, high intensity, and high excitement are the stuff of life. Boring. Mundane. Repetitive. Forgettable. And yet, we spend most of our lives on those things. We wash dishes, put them away, use them, start again. It's a repetitive life, this one.

The liturgy of the church is also an uneventful, repetitive thing. And it reminds me that there is grace and mercy in formulaic, repetitive worship. "The Lord be with you," says the priest. "And also with you," replies the congregation. Wash the dish, put it away, use it. While the moments of worship that are full of soul-moving, tear-jerking emotion are so very important, so is the liturgy, the rhythm, and the routine of reciting our praise and passing the peace. Perhaps what is ordinary is not, in fact, so ordinary. Perhaps there is glory, grace, and greatness in all of it.

 Name the tasks of your day that feel the most mundane. Remember that Jesus Himself came to earth not as a king, but as a baby in a manger. Glory, most high, in the least of us.

107

Late-Night Prayer Sessions

Do not be anxious about anything, but in every situation, by prayer and petition, with thanksgiving, present your requests to God.

PHILIPPIANS 4:6 NIV

Every day for a year, I woke up at 2:42 a.m. It was this weird occurrence that had no rhyme or reason, but it happened at exactly the same moment and kept me awake for at least an hour. My life those days was a blur of diapers, baby schedules, conference calls, and "Please advise ASAP" emails. I wasn't alone for more than a few minutes once the kids went to bed because I'd pass out as soon as my head hit the pillow.

In the beginning, I mentally thumbed through the pages of the proverbial book of *Things I Am Worried About, Didn't Finish, Forgot to Do, or May Never Do* that lived in my head. I need to change the oil in my car. I wonder if Brady has a cavity? That ache in my elbow is back . . . could it be (insert terminal illness)? I should cook more meals at home. My children may grow up to be totally damaged because I don't love to cook.

Every night was a "beat myself up" session. But then I started bringing those things up in prayer rather than ruminating on them. And things started to change. Instead of loathing those interruptions at 2:42 a.m., I gave my worries to God. I wondered if He was giving me that inner 2:42 a.m. alarm as a blessing. I began to fall back to sleep, waking up with a more peaceful heart; and eventually, the 2:42 a.m. inner alarm disappeared.

What have you been anxious about lately? During times of high stress, bring your thoughts to God.

One Small Step

*To do what is right and just is more acceptable to the L*ORD *than sacrifice.*

PROVERBS 21:3 NIV

Are you struggling to make a decision? Weighing the pros and cons between two choices or simply wondering what's next? So often we view these pivotal moments as grand decisions to be made, a hard *yes* or *no* in either direction. But that mindset can be overwhelming. Especially when we are still a few steps away from the pivot we have in mind.

Sometimes all we need to do is do the next right thing. This theory is used in recovery programs and is the title of an excellent book by Emily P. Freeman. So what, my friend, is the next right thing for you? Perhaps it's making a phone call. Maybe it's doing a little research. Sometimes the next right thing looks like simply making a list.

Wherever you are today, whether you are overwhelmed with your responsibilities or trying to discern between Door Number One and Door Number Two, consider what your next right thing may be. Remember, it might not be something you add to your day; it might be something you take away. It might be a nap or a break from the hustle or space in your schedule as you pray for wisdom and discernment.

What is your next right thing? Offer that step to God, and allow Him to assure you that sometimes the next right thing isn't as obvious as it may seem. Write down your thoughts on what those steps might be, pray over them, and see what the morning brings.

Live This Season Well

There is a time for everything, and a season for every
activity under the heavens: a time to be born and a time
to die, a time to plant and a time to uproot.

ECCLESIASTES 3:1–2 NIV

Sometimes we're called into a season of rest and replenishment, and sometimes we're called to put on our gloves and boots and tend the garden. To weed and till, plant and prune—to do work we're called to do, weariness aside. The harvest waits for no one.

And so, the way spring brings strawberries and summer brings corn, some seasons bring work and others bring rest. It's difficult to have one without the other. Night complements day. Warmth complements the cold. Sweet balances the savory. We need the joy of the young and the wisdom of the old.

So honor this season you're in, whatever it may be—whether grieving or celebrating, planning or producing, nurturing or remembering, working or resting. You'll never have this particular season again. Savor all that it is.

What season are you in right now? When were you in the opposite
season? What season do you think is coming next? How can you do
your very best during this particular time? Even in a season of work,
our daily rest is important to keep going. I pray, dear friend, that
tonight your sleep is sweet.

WEEK 13

Reflection

This week, we talked a lot about seasons and moving between them. Some seasons last days; others last years. What season of life are you in right now? Are you thriving or merely surviving? What does the next season look like for you? And what might your next step forward look like? Consider the following prompts:

In this season, I'm enjoying:

_____

_____

In this season, I'm challenged by:

_____

_____

In my next season, I hope:

_____

_____

_____

In my next season, I will ask God to help me:

_____

_____

_____

I pray your dreams are as lovely and calming as the sound sleep that finds you.

WEEK

14

. . . .

Step Away

*When I look at your heavens, the work of your fingers, the moon
and the stars, which you have set in place, what is man that you
are mindful of him, and the son of man that you care for him?*

PSALM 8:3-4

When you feel dried up, worn out, with not an ounce of creativity or thought-fulness left in your head, it's time to go outside. Everything works better when you unplug it for a little while. Your phone. Your computer. *You.*

Inside, we're surrounded by desks and chairs, lights and papers. But outside, we're surrounded by *creation.* Outside, our dreams can be as big as the sky, our tears as delicate as raindrops, our joy as pure and bright as sunshine. Don't worry about the weather. A mountain of joy can be found when you jump in mud puddles with bare feet. Lie in the grass. Take deep breaths of fresh air. In these moments, allow yourself to be replenished.

You weren't made to be caged. Holed up inside. Limited by ceilings and walls. You aren't refueled by loading that dishwasher again or sorting the mail or scrolling the headlines. Disconnect. Unplug. Go outside. Make a snowball. Jump in the lake. Have a picnic under the oak tree with crusty bread and creamy butter, with cheese and berries and a cold glass of iced tea.

There's something healing out there you won't find in here. Nature lets us see glimmers of heaven as we gaze upon the places God made with His own hands.

 Put this book down. Put your phone down. Wrap up in a blanket and go outside. Look up. Count the stars. Let the moon shine down on you. Let yourself be in awe of the universe.

Growing Goodness

The LORD will guide you always; he will satisfy your needs in a sun-scorched land and will strengthen your frame. You will be like a well-watered garden, like a spring whose waters never fail.

ISAIAH 58:11 NIV

Like many mothers, my friend Whitney experienced postpartum depression after the birth of her first child. Desperate for joy, aching to feel like herself again, she walked to her mailbox on a rainy, overcast day. Inside was a seed catalog she'd never ordered. The cover featured a beautiful bunch of zinnias in shades of pinks and corals. Gazing into her backyard, she had an idea. And so, her beautiful garden was born.

Whitney, a graphic designer by trade who can sit for long hours in front of a computer screen, began toiling in her backyard. She ordered seeds from the catalog and planted her first batch of flowers. Every morning, she brought her little one to the backyard to check on her plants while she enjoyed her coffee. As her flowers began to spring from the ground—first as little buds and later as big, beautiful blooms—so flourished Whitney's heart.

I think of Whitney's story often because I watched her journey firsthand. Intentionally shifting her focus away from the digital and toward something analog inspired every area of her life. What started as a handful of pots is now an expansive garden of flowers, vegetables, and more. Whitney's husband even built a free flower stand in their front yard to give blooms to neighbors.

Do you have any analog hobbies you enjoy? Is there a peaceful evening hobby you could incorporate into your life? Consider planning a walk tomorrow, phone-free. Using all your senses, take in your surroundings.

115

Pink Skies

But now, O LORD, you are our Father; we are the clay, and
you are our potter; we are all the work of your hand.

ISAIAH 64:8

I rode on an airplane for the very first time when I was nineteen years old. I was terrified and alone on my way to visit a friend. By the grace of God, I was seated next to a kind older man, a physician from our neighboring town. He explained every noise and every bump during takeoff and settled my fears quite a bit. It was only when we got above the clouds that I was able to bring myself to look out the window. The sun was just beginning to go down, and the blanket of clouds was tinted a bright orangey-pink, a color I'm convinced you can only see at 30,000 feet.

It took my breath away. *God, You are amazing*, I thought to myself.

Since that first airplane ride, I've always found God up there in the sky. It's a special treat, getting to see His handiwork from that perspective. It reminds me of how grand, how powerful, and how magnificent God is. Sometimes I put Him in a box labeled *church, prayers, and Bible study*. But He is so much bigger.

Where have you witnessed God's magnificence? Perhaps in the eyes of a new baby? Or from a mountaintop? Or maybe in the peace of a beloved grandmother near to heaven's gate? Spend a few minutes thinking about a moment you tucked into your heart.

A Prayer for Your Dreams

Oh, taste and see that the L\u0280\u1d0f\u0280\u1d05 is good! Blessed
is the man who takes refuge in him!

PSALM 34:8

. . . .

Tonight, I hold you in prayer and wish you an evening of rest and rejuvenation. I pray your dreams are whole and intact, that they're as lovely and calming as the sound sleep that finds you.

May their colors be vivid and beautiful, like art come to life. May the cast of characters be beloved friends, lost to the sands of time, and family venturing back to this side of heaven, just for a night. May their voices be soft, and may the background music be soothing. I pray your dreams are filled with mended fences, blooming friendships, and hopes come to life. Or back to life.

And most of all, I pray each one brings a smile to your face when you wake—a reminder of the sweet and the good in years past, and a hope for the days to come.

 Are your dreams reminding you of a worry or a hope you've pushed deep inside your heart? Is something rising to the surface, interrupting your rest? Give God the good and the worrisome before you head to sleep tonight.

Dulling of Delight

Count it all joy, my brothers, when you meet trials of various kinds.

JAMES 1:2

. . . .

To you, who are languishing. A friend recently told me that one of the most common feelings we experience after long periods of stress (like living through a pandemic, caring for a sick relative, or dealing with continual work stress) is the feeling of languishing.

A plant, for instance, languishes during a season of drought. In my own experience, languishing feels like I am the duck, swimming on top of the water. Above the water, all you see is the top half of me, perfectly poised. Below the water line, my legs kick and kick and kick, just trying to tread water.

During the pandemic, I heard psychologist Adam Grant explain more about *languishing*, a term I hadn't heard before in a mental health context. Adam explained, using research from sociologist Corey Keys, that when you're languishing, you often don't notice your drive begin to dull or dwindle. "You don't catch yourself slipping slowly into solitude," he said. "You're indifferent to your indifference. When you can't see your own suffering, you don't seek help or even do much to help yourself."

How are you doing today? Check in with yourself. Place your hand on your heart, and take a deep breath. Acknowledge what you've been through and what lies ahead. Acknowledge whatever emotion comes to the surface. Allow God's unshakable love and grace to wash over you.

 If you are languishing today, I pray flourishing is on the horizon for you. Find a friend or trusted advisor to talk to about your struggle. Then make a plan to try something new, to blossom and grow.

Reflection

This week, I talked a lot about inspiration. I find inspiration in my children, being outside, and in amazing books. Sometimes I'm inspired by music, especially the slow ballads. They just move my heart in a special way. What about you?

As we've reflected on God's magnificence in so many ways this week, where do you find inspiration?

_____

_____

_____

_____

_____

_____

_____

_____

_____

_____

_____

_____

_____

_____

_____

_____

_____

_____

When was the last time you were truly inspired? Describe that event here.

_____

_____

_____

_____

_____

_____

_____

_____

How do you feel when you're inspired? What's your mood like?

_____

_____

_____

_____

_____

_____

_____

_____

_____

How can you actively seek inspiration in your daily life? Could you take a dance class? Perhaps start a small garden in your yard? Or pick up a great book from the library?

_____
_____
_____
_____
_____
_____
_____
_____
_____
_____
_____
_____
_____
_____
_____
_____
_____

It's okay
to be in the
middle of your
journey.

WEEK

15

. . . .

Fanciest of the Fancy

You shall be a crown of beauty in the hand of the LORD,
and a royal diadem in the hand of your God.

ISAIAH 62:3

One of my grandmothers was a stay-at-home mom who raised five kids while her husband, my grandfather, traveled for work. She knew how to cook to feed a crowd and adopted every stray cat and dog that looked her way. My other grandmother was fancy. In fact, I would go so far as to say she was the fanciest of the fancy. I'll always remember her with her fur coat and white gloves, taking me to the nicest restaurant in town to practice table manners.

She loved a dinner party and never hesitated to set her long dining room table with the good china and all her best silver. She and my grandfather were known for graciously hosting elaborate dinner parties that stretched long into the evening.

Two very different women who loved their families relentlessly. Two different legacies of love. I'll always be grateful for the pieces of them that live on in me.

 What will your legacy be? A love of curiosity and travel? Or service to those in need? Your love for learning and books? Take a few minutes tonight to consider the legacy you're leaving. This is an intentional practice that's essential for purposeful living.

The Messy Middle

Your word is a lamp to my feet and a light to my path.

PSALM 119:105

I love a good before-and-after. Remember the television show *Extreme Makeover: Home Edition*? I loved curling up on a Sunday night to watch a home be utterly transformed in the span of sixty minutes. The big reveal always took my breath away. What a change! What a contrast! I loved the deep and special story told at the beginning and the way the middle sort of skipped along quickly, touching on the highlights of the journey but culminating in a big way at the end.

I don't know about you, but I'd much prefer my journeys through change to be so succinct. Let me have my story at the beginning, skip quickly through the middle, and relish the fantastic final result. Unfortunately, change doesn't work that way, does it?

The uncertainty, the discomfort, the messy middle—that's where growth happens. Not at the big reveal, and not even at the beginning. It's the in between, when the potter's clay is beginning to take shape but isn't recognizable as something good. That's just the way life goes. It's okay to be in the middle of your journey. Something good is happening, even if you can't see it yet.

Where are you in your journey? Are you closer to the beginning or closer to the end? Or are you somewhere in the murky, messy middle of it all? Wherever you are, be there wholeheartedly. Trust that God is working a masterpiece and that this is all an important part of the process.

Fruit of the Season

I am the vine; you are the branches. Whoever abides in me and I in him,
he it is that bears much fruit, for apart from me you can do nothing.

JOHN 15:5

My friend and coworker Jessa sent me a text the other day that absolutely stopped me in my tracks. She is an artist (the best of the best), a wife, and a mom to three children ages one to ten. We were talking about seasons of life and how it feels like some seasons yield more fruit than others.

"Yes," she replied to me. "But I'm learning that sometimes the fruits of my labor aren't for me. A tree doesn't consume its own fruit. Sometimes, our fruit is for others to enjoy or to fill a need in their life."

Wow.

As a mother, I feel that in my bones. I sometimes get lost in the consistent monotony of laundry, bills, grocery runs, and lunchboxes. And yet, reframing the truth of that statement, I am providing clean clothes for my children, feeding my tribe mostly healthy and delicious food, and keeping up with the tasks of maintaining a strong, safe, family home.

What beautiful fruit for all of us. Let me count it all joy to be chosen to serve in these ways, in this season. And let me remember those who went before me so that I may enjoy the fruits of their labor now.

What fruit is your season producing? For whom? How might you
reframe your thinking, both in gratitude and grace, about how God is
using you right now?

126

One of the Greatest Love Stories

Gray hair is a crown of glory; it is gained in a righteous life.

PROVERBS 16:31

When I was in college, I had the honor of sitting in a first-row seat to one of the greatest love stories ever told. No, it wasn't a production of Shakespeare or my own romantic endeavors. It was the sacrificial love of a daughter for her ailing, aging mother.

For twenty-two years, my grandmother had Alzheimer's, before the Lord called her home and cured her of this disease. And for twenty-two years, I watched my mom care for her mother the way she'd cared for me as a child: driving across town to pick her up for dinner at our house, baking cakes every Monday for the nursing home staff, showing up to do her hair and put on her lipstick every day after my mom left her job at a local elementary school.

It was true love in its greatest form: the gift of time, empathy, and deepest respect. My mom was there, ushering me into my grandmother's room in my graduation gown, and then later in my wedding gown so my grandmother could somewhat experience those milestones. My mom was there, refilling the bowl of peppermints for the nurses who stopped by. And she was there, holding my her hand, when my grandmother left this world for heaven. Love, at its absolute best.

Where have you seen the love of God played out in your life? Who embodies that for you? How might you step into that type of role now or in the future for someone else?

127

Poppy Seed Bread

Cast your burden on the Lord, and He shall sustain you.

PSALM 55:22 NKJV

. . . .

There are times in life when hope seems far away. When we are hurting so much, it's hard to see any sort of light at the end of the tunnel.

After my grandmother was diagnosed with Alzheimer's, she began to decline both quickly and slowly. Sometimes, it seemed as if she were getting better, or at least not getting any worse. Other times, she couldn't recognize us or remember our names. It was painful for all involved, especially my mom, who was her primary caregiver.

My grandmother had a deep love for a fancy poppy seed bread (a sweet dessert-type cake) from a local restaurant here in town. My mom would often stop after work to pick up a slice and bring it to her in the nursing home where she lived. Tears would well up in my mom's eyes while she helped feed her mom piece after piece. My grandmother would remark, "Oh, my favorite poppy seed bread!" And then a few minutes later, "Oh, my favorite poppy seed bread!" Each time she said it with a sweet, grateful smile.

Visiting with my mom one day as she fed my grandmother the poppy seed bread, I nudged her and said, "Look at the joy you're bringing her over and over." Sickness is awful. But joy is real.

 Until you've experienced the weight of darkness, it's hard to know how light joy can feel. My mom was experiencing both just moments apart. Have you ever seen slivers of light during a dark time? What did they mean to you?

128

Reflection

Legacy matters. The older we get, the more we start to think about the mark we're leaving on the world. Who has left a mark on your spirit? Is there someone in your life who's impacted who you've become in a positive way? What legacy do you hope to leave behind one day?

_____

_____

_____

_____

_____

_____

_____

_____

_____

_____

_____

_____

Be kind
to yourself.

WEEK

16

. . . .

He Is for You

For I consider that the sufferings of this present time are not worth comparing with the glory that is to be revealed to us.

ROMANS 8:18

For you, who are suffering.

Some suffering is clear—a cast on a broken arm or a bare scalp on someone struggling with cancer. For others, their suffering is hidden. It's the ache buried deep inside. It's the grief silently shouldered alone. It's the depression that blankets the otherwise happy life with sadness.

Whether your suffering is clear or silent, you are not alone. You are worthy of love and joy. God is for you, not against you. Have faith that the next step forward is the right step toward wholeness; and along the way, you'll be draped in the warm love of God. Be kind to yourself. Like a person with a broken leg, move carefully and slowly. Allow yourself extra time to do the ordinary things of life. Give yourself extra sleep, nourishment, and rest. Seek God's truth in this season, and allow His love to be a balm to your aching heart.

Pray with me:
Lord, I am weary. I am suffering, and this suffering hurts. I lay it at Your feet and ask for Your guidance as I take my next step forward. Lead me to truth, light, and joy. In Jesus' holy name. Amen.

DAY 77

Heroes and Helpers

"I have said these things to you, that in me you may have peace. In the world you will have tribulation. But take heart; I have overcome the world."

JOHN 16:33

My mom burst into my room one day when I was a child. It was one of those days that mark a life. Slicing through the ordinary with something extraordinary, marking the end of the Before and the beginning of the After.

"There's been an accident," she said.

We rushed out the door. Arriving at the hospital, we learned that my dad, who'd been out on his maiden voyage with his brand-new boat (a dream he'd had since he was a child), had been injured by a fishing leader, the long, pointy part of a fishing hook. On the way to the hospital, he'd removed it from his left eye. What followed was a series of wins and losses, successful surgeries, and an eventual 360-degree retinal detachment, leaving my dad blind in his left eye.

While my dad was so brave and handled this tragedy with his trademark sense of humor and steadfast confidence, the hero of the story was my little brother. Brett was only thirteen when the accident happened, and he was on the boat at the time. He remained calm. He helped swiftly and carefully. And, having never driven anything before, he drove the new boat all the way back to the dock to get my dad the care he needed.

Though this event was so tragic, the steadfast bravery of my dad and my brother reminded me that I, too, can be brave in the face of hardship.

What milestone markers dot the timeline of your life? Who were the heroes of those stories, and how have they shaped your life?

133

Upside Down

The Lord is near to the brokenhearted and saves the crushed in spirit. Many are the afflictions of the righteous, but the Lord delivers him out of them all.

PSALM 34:18–19

There are days when we wake up and the world is one way . . . and then we go to sleep with the knowledge that life will never be the same. These days are markers in our lives, flagging the beginning of the After, the end of the Before. Sometimes these are happy days, days we will treasure forever. But sometimes, these are sad days. The day of the phone call, the diagnosis, the accident, or the day you said goodbye.

For you, whose world is turned upside down—a blessing:

> You are seen. You are known. Your heavenly Father has come before you here and made a way. You are not forgotten or forsaken. May you know, deep in your heart, that God loves you with a love unlike any you can ever know.

> You are not alone. Though darkness falls, the morning will soon come again. And while it is dark, God will stand watch. He will not slumber or sleep.

> You are loved. You are here. You will find a way ahead. God has forged this path already and will walk alongside you as you travel it. When you are weak, He is strong.

 If your world has turned upside down, allow yourself the grace to sit in the now. God is forging love out of hurt, joy out of grief, and faith out of fear.

Without Ceasing

He who watches over you will not slumber.

PSALM 121:3 NIV

Tonight, I want to leave you with a beautiful piece of scripture to tuck deep inside your heart as you go off to sleep. I love how simply and beautifully the writer details God's promises of protection both day and night. We can rest assured that He is keeping watch, giving us the gift of peaceful sleep and recuperation.

> I lift up my eyes to the mountains—where does my help come from?
> My help comes from the LORD, the Maker of heaven and earth.
> He will not let your foot slip—he who watches over you will not
>   slumber;
> Indeed, he who watches over Israel will neither slumber nor sleep.
> The LORD watches over you—the LORD is your shade at your
>   right hand;
> the sun will not harm you by day, nor the moon by night.
> The LORD will keep you from all harm—he will watch over your life;
> the LORD will watch over your coming and going both now and
>   forevermore. (Psalm 121 NIV)

What part of Psalm 121 stands out to you the most? Did you know the Lord never sleeps? I found this note to be particularly meaningful. His love and protection are truly never-ending.

135

For You, Who Feel Alone in the Night

He heals the brokenhearted and binds up their wounds.

PSALM 147:3 NIV

Once the sun sets and the noises of the world begin to quiet, do you ever feel lonely? I think we all have at one time or another. Perhaps you live alone. Maybe you live with a partner or a family, but you still feel those emotions surfacing in the dark of night.

For you, who are silently crushed in spirit and aching for companionship and love, a special blessing:

> May you remember that you are altogether wonderfully made and worthy of love of all kinds, just as you are.

> I pray that while you are in this season, you find joy and togetherness in unexpected places: an impromptu invitation from a friend, books full of magnificent, complex characters, or a neighbor who pops by for a visit.

> May you be filled with the love of God who cherishes every bit of who you are and who you are not. May you find yourself strengthened by the knowledge that God is with you, for you, and near you always.

Go easy on yourself. If you are lonely, perhaps you can show yourself some extra love tonight? A quiet bubble bath. A warm cup of tea. A good book. An early bedtime.

Reflection

This week, we leaned into the concept of suffering and how growth and faith are sometimes born from our most painful moments. While these memories aren't all that fun to look back on, I think it's important to acknowledge how they marked our path and may have played pivotal roles in our development.

What has suffering looked like for you?

_____

_____

_____

_____

_____

_____

_____

_____

_____

_____

_____

_____

_____

_____

_____

How did God meet you in that pain?

_____

_____

_____

_____

_____

_____

Is there an experience in your life that impacted who you are more than others?

_____

_____

_____

_____

_____

_____

_____

_____

_____

If you are suffering now, remember this: God has not forgotten you. He is for you. He is with you. He is steady when you are coming undone. He is near when you feel so far away. He is preparing goodness ahead for you.

Use this space to journal your thoughts and feelings.

_____

_____

_____

_____

_____

_____

_____

_____

_____

_____

_____

_____

_____

_____

_____

_____

_____

_____

Discover God in the Ordinary.

WEEK

17

· · · · · · · · · · · · · · · · · · ·

When Hurricanes Hit

He made the storm be still, and the waves of the sea were hushed.

PSALM 107:29

In the late-night hours of September 16, 2020, Hurricane Sally hit Pensacola, Florida. Huddled in sleeping bags in our primary bedroom, our kids tried to sleep while Bryan and I paced the dark, powerless house watching for leaks. Since I'm a Florida native, hurricanes are nothing new to me, but the wind and rain raged that night in a way I'd never seen before. Terrified, but attempting to remain calm for the kids, we played card games by flashlight and counted the minutes until dawn.

The next morning, after none of us had slept, we emerged from our hideaway to see total and utter destruction around us. Homes flooded. Roofs torn off. Trees lying on their sides, blocking any vehicles from getting by. We found oysters and fish in our yard because the water had come up so high. More than twenty barges had gotten loose in Pensacola Bay, and one had wedged itself into a yard half a mile away.

And yet, the helpers began to emerge. Neighbors with chainsaws walked the streets and helped where they could. A friend delivered coffee from her stove-top coffee pot via a golf cart. Homes with generators were opened up for showers and air conditioning. During our time of despair, we saw the very best of people. True friendship, helping hands, and service done in love.

 When has God shown Himself to you during your time of need? While experiencing tragedy or tough times, have you experienced this type of goodness? How has it shaped your view of the world?

On Love and Luck

See, I am doing a new thing! Now it springs up; do you not perceive it?
I am making a way in the wilderness and streams in the wasteland.

ISAIAH 43:19 NIV

My family loves the very Southern tradition of eating a great big meal together, midday, every New Year's Day.

Like clockwork, every year my mom digs in her purse and pulls out a dime. She scrubs it clean, dries it off, and drops it into a great big pot of black-eyed peas. The kids, and even the adults, take turns making our plates in the kitchen, carefully scooping our black-eyed peas onto our plates, hoping to be "the lucky one." See, if you find the dime in your black-eyed peas, you are guaranteed to have the luckiest year. Inevitably, someone is caught peeking through the pot, trying to get the perfect scoop, and they get in trouble. After we say the blessing, everyone digs in. "I got it!" someone will yell, and we all cheer for them. Smiles are exchanged, and the tradition is set aside until next year.

This year, after my daughter was crowned "the lucky one," I looked around the table and smiled. This tradition reminds me how "lucky" we are to have people to love and who love us in return. However silly some of our traditions might be, I love this reminder to stop and be grateful.

Tonight, let's fill our hearts with a spirit of gratitude, thankful for ordinary moments and the loved ones who fill them.

Gratitude changes everything. Who are you most grateful for this evening? What ordinary moments happened today that make your life abundantly blessed?

143

Be Patient

He has made everything beautiful in its time.
ECCLESIASTES 3:11 NIV

· ·

Today the well feels dry. I ache to create art, to be divinely inspired and make something special and wonderful. There's magic when that happens: When words come together in just the right way to stir feeling into your soul. When colors and brushstrokes fit, together creating beauty where there was none. When a meal is pulled from the oven perfectly browned, lightly crispy and fragrant, inviting everyone to partake in its bounty. Those magic-maker moments are rare. They're glimpses into heaven, gifts from the great Maker.

Patience and consistency are integral parts of every artist's process, whatever that art may be. These are the hardest parts to embrace, if you ask me. I often want to manufacture a moment or believe art into existence, but beauty happens at God's perfect time. For the artist, patience means practicing. Practicing the thing God placed in your heart, be it cooking, sewing, writing, painting, piano playing, gardening, home decorating, and even parenting.

Consistently returning to our art, our craft, or putting pen to paper creates an invitation for the magic to come. But with this patience and consistency, we must also rest and give God space to renew us.

May your rest tonight be sweet, my friend. And may you awaken tomorrow with fresh inspiration, with water flowing in your well to be a vessel of God's beauty in the world.

  What is your creative outlet? How does it bring you life?

Collecting Words

Let your speech always be gracious, seasoned with salt, so that
you may know how you ought to answer each person.

COLOSSIANS 4:6

For as long as I can remember, I've been a collector of words. Words put together in just the right way, quotes that shine a light on the human experience, stories that bring us together as one. I have a note on my phone where I jot them down—beautiful words that I read, phrases that come to me in the produce section of the grocery store, a story told to me by my seatmate on an airplane, concepts that pop up while I'm working that I want to unravel. It's a beautiful thing to both read and write words, to experience thoughts that touch hearts and make me think, *Oh wow . . . me too.*

I'll often pull out my collection of wonderful words when I'm writing a story or sending a note to a friend or explaining something important to my kids. It's my hope that a piece of my collection helps an idea click into place for a reader or makes a friend feel better or opens the heart of a child.

Collecting beautiful words and ideas could be a soothing nighttime routine. Consider making yourself a cup of tea, curling up with a blanket, and jotting down some favorite words, quotes, or Bible verses you would like to return to. You can even quote your family and friends.

Start a note on your phone or a list in your journal. Begin the practice of collecting words of inspiration, encouragement, and promises of truth.

Faith of a Child

He called a little child to him, and placed the child among them. And he said: "Truly I tell you, unless you change and become like little children, you will never enter the kingdom of heaven. Therefore, whoever takes the lowly position of this child is the greatest in the kingdom of heaven."

MATTHEW 18:2-4 NIV

Do you long to feel and experience God in a deeply personal way? I understand that feeling. But I've found that I tend to see God in moments that are so ordinary and, yet, almost too profound and treasured to describe with words. When I begin to list these moments, I feel God so near to me. It's a practice I've gone back to over and over when I feel like I've fallen out of sync with His will for me or when I long for a deeper connection with Him.

And so, I start to look around with a glad and grateful heart. I don't usually see Him in giant things like trophies or achievements or rainbows, though I know He's in all of that too. I see God's grace and abiding love for me in quiet moments of regular life. Bread and butter, butterfly kisses from a child, a peck on the cheek as you run out the door—I think He wants us to look there too.

If you're struggling with a complicated faith, I invite you to the childlike practice of discovering God in the ordinary.

Children often engage in the simple but sacred practice of a bedtime prayer. Let's not allow our busy adulthood to abandon that. Tonight, before you sleep, say your prayers, and ask God to walk with you, revealing Himself in the sacred practices of daily life.

Reflection

To live with gratitude is to live wholeheartedly with our eyes wide open. And yet, it is sometimes difficult to be grateful for certain challenges or troubles in life. What are you grateful for at the end of this week? Is there someone who made your week a little better? Was there a tough situation you're thankful to have experienced and come through? What small joys are you grateful for this week?

_____

_____

_____

_____

_____

_____

_____

_____

_____

_____

_____

_____

_____

You are more than the sum of your checkmarks.

WEEK

18

· ·

When You Feel Stuck, Change Your Ways

The LORD is my rock and my fortress and my deliverer, my God, my rock, in whom I take refuge, my shield, and the horn of my salvation, my stronghold.

PSALM 18:2

. . . .

"I just feel stuck." I've said this a few times in my life. One time was particularly tough. Lying on my bed, facedown. Crying because everything was hard. Everything was busy. And nothing would give. Bryan, as he often does, tried to talk me out of my slump. "Cheer up," he said, always the carefree optimist. "Look at the bright side," he encouraged. (I love him for this.) But in my mind, everything was on fire, and no one had water.

"You've got to get out of your head," he finally said to me one day. "You're going to stay stuck until you start turning over the rocks keeping you there. Flip them over. Question all of them. Anything is possible. You have to be willing to fight your way out of the hole, or you're going to stay stuck exactly where you are."

And so I did. Instead of trying to arrange the puzzle pieces of my life to fit exactly as they were, all complicated and giant, I looked at my life like a slate wiped clean. Then slowly, I started adding back the most important pieces, finding new ways to work them into my schedule. But this time, I did it in the proper order: what mattered most went in first.

Is it time for you to take a second look at your commitments? Are you feeling stuck where you are? Ask God to help you discern what belongs on your plate and what doesn't.

Preparation for Success

The plans of the diligent lead surely to abundance.

PROVERBS 21:5

. . . .

In the evenings, once the kids are in bed, I like to tidy up for the next day. I also like to do a few things to set myself up for success once the new day begins. I'll share a few of my own preparation tips as well as some from readers below:

- Prep the coffee pot to automatically brew at the desired morning time.
- Run the dishwasher so it's ready to be emptied in the morning.
- Pack lunchboxes and prepare water bottles for the next day.
- Set the timer on the washing machine so the load is ready for the dryer in the morning.
- Lay out your outfit for the next day or gather workout clothes and shoes so no decisions need to be made.
- Make sure your purse or backpack is packed and ready to go for the day ahead.

 Perhaps these suggestions will spark a few "morning prep" ideas that will work for your season. Trust me: your future self will thank you.

Dear Diary

*And the L*ORD* answered me: "Write the vision; make it*
plain on tablets, so he may run who reads it."

HABAKKUK 2:2

When you were little, did you ever keep a diary? Maybe it was a fluffy pink thing with a fake-gold lock and key. Or maybe it was a handful of notebook paper stuffed in the back of your nightstand.

My daughter has one. She tells me she writes about her favorite stuffed animals, which Squishmallow plushie she wants for Christmas, and sometimes about her favorite babysitters. My best friend's grandmother kept a journal—many journals, actually. She detailed her travels around the world: where she stayed, what she ate, who she met. They are family treasures now. However you keep records of your comings and goings, journaling helps us unburden our minds and get our thoughts onto paper.

I often find that once I get my thoughts on paper, I'm better able to critically think through them. I can see what's taking up my brain space and compartmentalize the thoughts when they're all visible. If you struggle with journaling or knowing what to write about, here are a few ideas to get you started:

- Outline your day. What you did, where you went, who you met.
- Brain dump your thoughts. Get everything out of your head.
- List three things you're grateful for.
- Note the best moment of your day and the most challenging.
- Write out a prayer.

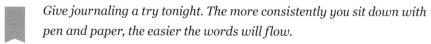

Give journaling a try tonight. The more consistently you sit down with pen and paper, the easier the words will flow.

Give Your Best Yes

*Again I saw that under the sun the race is not to the swift, nor the battle
to the strong, nor bread to the wise, nor riches to the intelligent, nor favor
to those with knowledge, but time and chance happen to them all.*

ECCLESIASTES 9:11

. . . .

I often stop to think that if I hadn't answered that late phone call on that fateful
night back in 2007 . . . if I hadn't said yes when a friend asked if I wanted to
meet up . . . if I hadn't said hello to the boy from the restaurant where I used
to work . . . I would have never married Bryan Ley. I'd have never become
Brady, Tyler, and Caroline's mom. So much of my life would look unbelievably
different.

As an extroverted introvert, I have a tendency to stay in my bubble. To stay
safely inside my circle of friends, my favorite spots in town, my work that I
know is safe and secure. And yet, what if saying yes to something outside my
comfort zone could be my best yes yet? Some things happen to us, but some
things happen because we put ourselves out there.

*When have you put yourself out there in a brave way? Has one yes
altered the course of your life? Is there a decision you're trying to make
now that might benefit from your courage? What could it mean for the
rest of your life?*

153

For You, Whose Work Is Never Done

A joyful heart is good medicine, but a crushed spirit dries up the bones.

PROVERBS 17:22

Whether you're caring for a new baby, a sick child, an aging parent, or nurturing the work you love (or all of the above), some days can feel like the work is never done. I often find it hard to go to sleep when all my tasks haven't been checked off my to-do list. It feels like I can only draw my day to a close when I'm able to shut the book on that list. But what is a life when it's lived chasing after a list?

I hope you'll take a deep breath and receive this blessing tonight:

> May you give yourself a moment to take a few deep breaths. May the Lord guide you to the reason you work as hard as you do. And may the knowledge that He's working and watching out for you bring peace to your racing heart.

> May you remember that life is more than lists. Life is moments connected by time and love: a hand slipped slowly into yours on a walk, the joy of a puppy, bedtime prayers recited together.

> May you never give yourself so wholeheartedly to your lists that you forget to live your life. You are more than the sum of your check marks.

Consider tomorrow's to-dos. What can you rearrange or move to make space for life to happen? These are the moments that will fuel your energy and passion for the work you must do.

Reflection

This week, we discussed the tactics of planning ahead. As you've probably learned from experience, setting yourself up for success at night often means you're in for a fantastic morning. As this week draws to a close and you set your sights on the week ahead, how might you prepare yourself and your home for a steady-paced, organized, peaceful seven days ahead? Tactically, let's break this plan down into categories. Think through each area, then create a task list.

MEALS

What are your goals for meals this week? Eat healthy? Be quick and efficient? A mixture of both?

_____

_____

_____

_____

_____

_____

_____

_____

HOUSEWORK

Where does the laundry currently stand? What chores need to be completed? Can some of these be delegated to other members of your family?

_____

_____

_____

_____

_____

_____

SCHEDULE

How does the next week look? A loose schedule or a tight timeline? Can anything move to create some margin?

_____

_____

_____

_____

_____

_____

REST

How will you care for your mind, body, and spirit this next week?
This matters.

_____

_____

_____

_____

_____

_____

_____

_____

_____

_____

_____

_____

_____

_____

_____

Jesus,
I give
You my plans
& pray Your
will be done.

WEEK

19

. . . .

Best-Laid Plans

Many are the plans in the mind of a man, but it is the purpose of the LORD that will stand.

PROVERBS 19:21

. . . .

I've spent many a Sunday setting lofty goals and attempting to revamp nearly every area of my life. *This week, I will be healthier! I will manage my finances better! I will exercise every single day!* You see where this is going . . .

Once, I spent a week organizing and labeling a giant, poster-sized calendar in my office. It was color-coded, fully planned out, and made me feel like the most organized person on Earth. And then a pandemic happened, and all my plans came to a screeching halt.

The world around us changed. Businesses shut their doors. Hand sanitizer was in short supply. People hoarded toilet paper. People were frantic to stock up, to make quick decisions. Here in our home, though, we hunkered down. Sure, like everyone, we cancelled hotel rooms, learned how to log in to Zoom classrooms, and ordered masks from Amazon. But we also slowed our pace, turned our attention inward. It was a forced change of pace, but a deeply impactful one. Suddenly, home became very, very important. It was our school, our church, our workplace, our vacation, all at once.

I know what it is to cling to my best-laid plans. I also know what it is to surrender them. Pray with me tonight: *Jesus, I give You my plans. I trust You with them and pray Your will be done. Amen.*

How was your day-to-day life impacted by the pandemic? What did your family learn during the slower pace of life? Were there good things in that slower pace you should return to?

Together and Apart

Two are better than one, because they have a good reward for their toil. For if they fall, one will lift up his fellow. But woe to him who is alone when he falls and has not another to lift him up! Again, if two lie together, they keep warm, but how can one keep warm alone? And though a man might prevail against one who is alone, two will withstand him—a threefold cord is not quickly broken.

ECCLESIASTES 4:9–12

I love a quiet movie night at home—kids scattered along the couches, snuggled under blankets, the smell of popcorn in the air. I'd take a quiet night at home over a night out any day. This is what makes me feel safe and secure. And those feelings matter—especially when the world outside these walls seems to be changing every second, the news keeps getting scarier, and the concerns of the world are becoming heavier (especially as my children get older). But here, with my old leopard blanket in my lap, a kid or two (or three) crammed onto the couch with me, and my husband searching for the perfect movie—this is home.

Do you have a place or people that feel like home to you? Are you reaping the benefits of togetherness with them, or are you overfilling your plate with other priorities? We make time for dentist appointments and soccer practice, but sometimes we forget to pencil in time with our people. That "fill my cup" type togetherness that leaves us feeling loved, connected, and rested. How might you be more intentional about filling your calendar with these types of commitments?

How are you making time and space for moments of connection in your life? With your partner, your family, your friends? Do you feel balanced in this area, or could it use some attention?

To Love and Be Loved

"For God so loved the world, that He gave His only Son, so that everyone who believes in Him will not perish, but have eternal life."

JOHN 3:16 NASB

February is a special month in our house. My mom, my sister-in-law, my son, and I—we were all born in February. My oldest son was born on February 16 after nine harrowing months of fear. At eighteen weeks pregnant, our doctor who specialized in high-risk pregnancies explained to us that he had several concerns about Brady. He informed us that we'd need weekly checkups but would not know if Brady was healthy—or if he'd even survive—until he was born.

I spent the following months paralyzed by fear, anger, and helplessness. I pleaded with God to save our son. He'd been long prayed for, and I already loved him with my entire being.

On February 16 at 7:21 p.m., I was lying on an operating room table. And with my husband at my side, I let tears fall from my eyes, and I turned my palms upward in surrender. I loved my baby. I trusted God. I would follow God's lead. I silently recited John 3:16 while my healthy, beautiful baby was gently delivered into the world. This experience was a turning point for me. A moment I will never forget.

What pivotal moments has your life held? How have they played a role in your personal growth?

Borrow this prayer:
Dear God, sometimes I cannot fathom how You could love us so much—to give Your one and only Son so that we may have everlasting life. Thank You for loving me so completely. Amen.

Love Is a Choice

However, let each one of you love his wife as himself, and
let the wife see that she respects her husband.

EPHESIANS 5:33

Do you have a person in your life you love wholeheartedly, but your relationship isn't always 100 percent perfect? Perhaps a best friend or a spouse? As little girls, we dream of fairy-tale relationships that survive on the sheer bliss of new love. And best friendships that are easy as pie because you have so much in common. But I have learned that isn't the case as time goes on. Our most important relationships require not just love and affection from us, but attention and, well, work.

Lasting love requires a choice, minute after minute. We choose our person and their well-being over and over again—in the face of disagreement, difficulties, and more. We choose our words carefully to honor their feelings. We choose to communicate with respect, even when we are upset. We choose our person when they are at their best and when they are not.

Who is your person? Perhaps your spouse, your partner, or a dear friend. What strengths does your relationship have? What weaknesses? What opportunities are there for you to work on your communication, your disagreement style, or your respect for them?

 How can you choose your person today? What's one way you can honor them in your daily actions moving forward?

A Trusted Resource

There is therefore now no condemnation to those who are in Christ Jesus.

ROMANS 8:1 NKJV

When I was a kid, my parents were honest with my brother and me about the facts of life, answering our questions and fielding our concerns. At one point, a limit was put on the number of questions I could ask in a day. I had many. I wanted to know it all.

Now I have three kids who ask a million questions a day. But I honor them, respecting their curiosities and promising to always tell them the truth in an age-appropriate way. I want them to know Bryan and I are their trusted resource. Not the television. Not the internet. Not their friends.

As an adolescent, I took some pretty big questions to my parents that my friends didn't dare take to theirs. About boys and first love, about popularity and jealousy, and about my changing body. They stripped away the shame and fear from the conversation. They made space for my feelings, respecting them, and promising to share truths with me. Because my parents were so accepting and encouraging of this level of communication, I now feel comfortable taking all my awkwardness, my anxiety, my questions, and my greatest fears to God. He strips away the shame. He makes space for my feelings. And the truth . . . it's there too. He meets me with it when I come to Him.

Are you sometimes fearful to tell God the truth? To acknowledge the things that wake you in the middle of the night, the worries that slowly simmer in the back of your mind? Take those to Him tonight. He's here. He's listening.

Reflection

How good God is to give us community. To allow us to do life with one another. It truly takes a village to be a human. We learn so much from each other, and we experience so much together. So who is your village? How might you pray for them today? Lift them and their situations up to the Lord so that you might honor those most important to you.

God is
always a
soft place to
land, even as
we grow.

WEEK

20

Trunks, Bodies, and Tails

A fool takes no pleasure in understanding, but only in expressing his opinion.

PROVERBS 18:2

I heard a story once about an elephant and three blind men. Each man was asked to touch one part of the elephant and describe what he was touching. The man touching the trunk thought he was touching a slithery snake. The man touching the body described a wall. The man holding the tail told everyone he was holding a rope. None of the men were correct, but each described his personal experience with what he was touching based on his individual perspective.

We approach life with the perspective of our unique experiences. And into every situation, we bring the scars and the knowledge gained from every moment we've lived before then. We all approach the same issues from different angles.

When we shift the angle of our vantage points—perhaps holding the tail or moving to the body—we begin to understand the bigger picture. Sometimes, it's imperative to consider a situation from all angles.

 What issue is currently on your mind? How has your perspective been shaped by where you've been and where you currently stand? Is there a different viewpoint you've missed and might consider?

Life-Giving

By wisdom a house is built, and by understanding it is established; by knowledge the rooms are filled with all precious and pleasant riches.

PROVERBS 24:3–4

My friend Sally Clarkson and her daughter, Sarah, wrote a book that changed my life. It's called *The Lifegiving Home: Creating a Place of Belonging and Becoming*. In it, Sally discusses how she created a home that was more than "just a place to stash your stuff."

Home, to me, is a place of warmth, peace, nourishment, and calm. Candles lit, flickering on tables as the sun goes down. A basket of soft blankets near the sofa. A bowl of candy on the coffee table to surprise and delight. The sound of music softening the atmosphere. Art and mementos inviting conversation about the past and inspiring thoughts about the future.

I tended to notice these things in the homes of others, but I didn't realize just how important these details were. Sally's wisdom inspired me to take a fresh look at my home and see what I could do to make our space more comfortable and special. What a joy to be able to do this. No matter the size or shape of our homes, we have the ability to make them places where we can truly rest and belong.

 Is your home life-giving or life-draining? Think of a gathering spot in your home. How can you make it a little extra cozy? What other ways can you shape your home to be one that fuels the people who live inside it?

Seeking Delight

For the L ORD takes delight in his people; he crowns the humble with victory.

PSALM 149:4 NIV

Are there things in your life that just bring a smile to your face? Perhaps your dog, your kid's silly dance moves, or that feeling you get when you play the piano? Well, I have long been a loyal fan of the US Navy Blue Angels. Their precision, their power, and the formality of it all. It's just amazing and always makes me jump to my feet. My love for them is rooted in our family tradition of watching them every summer and fall.

On a random Wednesday in August, a friend who worked with the Blue Angels invited my family to watch a practice show. Though I was desperately busy with work, I jumped at the chance.

That afternoon, we watched the Blue Angels practice up close (from the actual flight line!). It was a few hours full of joy and delight. Perhaps the most productive thing I'd done all week. Sometimes we think work really moves the needle forward on our lives, when often it's our choices to seek joy that do it instead.

How can you actively seek delight today? An up-close airshow may not be in the cards for your near future, but can you allow yourself a few minutes to experience a little bit of joy? What will it be?

Love and Growth

Keep me as the apple of your eye; hide me in the shadow of your wings.

PSALM 17:8 NIV

Do you have a relationship in your life that is so tender, it's hard to navigate sometimes? Maybe a child you love so much and are learning how to be near, but not *so* near that you inhibit her or his growth?

My oldest is twelve going on forty. He has an old soul, a deep tenderness to him, and a spirit of quiet leadership through and through. He flexes his muscles and spreads his wings, sometimes bumping up against boundaries he hadn't yet realized or rules we quickly put in place to catch up with his maturing. To me, he is still my Brady Bear, two years old and my favorite companion—though he would not approve of that name these days. I want to baby and love him with all of me until he is ninety-four, but I'm learning he needs love . . . and he also needs a little bit more. He needs freedom and room to grow and learn.

It's so enormous—the responsibility and privilege to love a child and get them prepared to launch into the world. And so we go about this delicate dance of holding on, pulling close, and letting go.

I often think it's a metaphor for how God loves us. He teaches. He helps us course correct. He pulls us near. He's always there. And He's always a soft place to land, even as we grow.

 Does this idea of love and growth ring true for you? Do you see God's love mirrored in your love for someone special? How can you more closely mirror His unconditional love in your own relationships?

DAY 100

Near in the Night

Give thanks in all circumstances; for this is the
will of God in Christ Jesus for you.

1 THESSALONIANS 5:18

. . . .

What a journey this has been! One hundred days studying, learning about, and discovering God's nearness to us during the night. By now, you've probably begun to understand that *night*, in this sense, can mean the time between dusk and twilight, when the sun disappears behind the horizon and the stars come out. And it can also mean a dark night of the soul—a difficult, dry season. A period of loneliness, sadness, or emptiness.

Whatever *night* means to you right now, I hope you've seen the beauty of God's proximity during these particular times. When we are lonely, He is near to us. When we are sad, He is there to remind us of the good and the light in the world (and in each other). When we are lost, He is there to remind us of the way back home (and back to ourselves). What a beautiful gift.

I invite you to use our last evening together to reflect on what you've learned. How God has come closer to you through these last twenty weeks. He is for you. He never forgets. His love is steadfast, constant, and near.

Borrow this prayer:
Lord, thank You for the ways You've come close to me through this
journey. I know the sun can't shine all the time—and that dark days
and nights will surely find me. Please remind me, always, that You are
near and that I have nothing to fear with You by my side. Thank You
for loving me wholly, without fail. Amen.

WEEK 20
Reflection

CLOSING THOUGHTS

Hi, friend! Here we are, wrapping up one hundred days together. Tonight, I invite you to reflect on all this experience has held for you. Take inventory of where you've been so that you might make tweaks and adjustments to move forward boldly, intentionally, and with gratitude.

UPS: What achievements, big or small, have you made so far?

_____

_____

_____

_____

_____

_____

_____

_____

_____

_____

DOWNS: What stumbling blocks or mistakes have occurred?

_____

_____

_____

_____

_____

_____

_____

_____

_____

LEARNING: Through the ups and the downs, what is God teaching you about Himself and about yourself?

_____

_____

_____

_____

_____

_____

_____

LOOKING AHEAD: What hopes do you have for the coming days?

_____

_____

_____

_____

_____

_____

_____

_____

Considering your answers to these questions, I invite you to spend some time quieting your heart and mind before God. I have a few reminders for you:

- **UPS**: You have permission to celebrate every victory no matter how private, tiny, or nuanced it might be. Every inch forward is momentum.
- **DOWNS**: You are not defined by your downs. They are part of the human experience. You are neither too much nor not enough. Grace upon grace.
- **LEARNING**: You know what He's teaching you, even if it's hard to learn. Lean in. Allow His purpose to unfold, no matter what it may require from you.
- **LOOKING AHEAD**: Boldly believe in God's promises: God designed you for a purpose (Ephesians 2:10). God will strengthen and help you (Isaiah 41:10). God can be trusted (Hebrews 10:23).

A Prayer of Gratitude

Lord, thank You for the ways You're turning my heart back to You. Thank You for cracking my heart wide open so that I can feel the ways You're working in my life with more clarity. Thank You for pursuing me day in and day out, even when I run away. You're always there, even when I want to hide. Thank You for being the steadfast, unchanging truth in this ever-changing world. I know deep in my soul it is You I can count on, at all times, through all things. You are my rock, my fortress, and my salvation.

The worries of my heart—even the ones I dare not speak aloud—I give to You. Help me face the fears and sins I have tried to ignore. Help me become the person You made me to be. Make use of every good day, every bad day, and every ordinary moment in between. Thank You for being near me as I venture down this road. In Your holy name I pray. Amen.

A Benediction

May God reveal Himself to you in clear and poignant ways.

May He help you tune in to the sound of His voice so that you might hear His will for your days.

May you always remember that you are deeply, entirely, and fully loved just as you are.

Scriptures for Your Evening

The LORD is your keeper; the LORD is your shade on your right hand. The sun shall not strike you by day, nor the moon by night. The LORD will keep you from all evil; he will keep your life.

PSALM 121:5-7

In peace I will both lie down and sleep; for you alone, O LORD , make me dwell in safety.

PSALM 4:8

If you lie down, you will not be afraid; when you lie down, your sleep will be sweet.

PROVERBS 3:24

I lay down and slept; I woke again, for the LORD sustained me.

PSALM 3:5

He will not let your foot be moved; he who keeps you will not slumber. Behold, he who keeps Israel will neither slumber nor sleep.

PSALM 121:3-4

Do not be anxious about anything, but in everything by prayer and supplication with thanksgiving let your requests be made known to God. And the peace of God, which surpasses all understanding, will guard your hearts and your minds in Christ Jesus.

PHILIPPIANS 4:6-7

Evening Routines

Drawing your day to a close with grace and intention can impact your sleep, your anxiety, and your health in enormous ways. Not only will you fall asleep faster with a consistent, relaxing evening routine, but your mornings will also run smoother as you've already prepared for the day ahead.

Evening routines are made of two parts. First, you care for your body by preparing it for rest. Second, you use the energy and time you have now to prepare for the morning to come. One is internal intention, and one is external intention.

PREPARING YOUR BODY FOR REST

Never underestimate the power of mood lighting. Seriously. When the work of the day is done, dim the lights to signal to your brain that it's time to slow down. I usually do this a few hours before bedtime, just as the sun begins to go down. Sometimes, I'll light a few candles as well.

Taking time to shower and do all the steps of your favorite skincare routine will also help you feel your best as you go to sleep. If there are "tools" to your sleeping trade (a weighted blanket, a linen spray, white noise, a fan), get those ready in advance too.

You've heard me say this before, and I'll say it again: writing down your routine will help it go from task list to habit. The more you can do to help your body feel clean, refreshed, and calm before bed, the quicker sleep will find you.

PREPARING FOR THE MORNING

Consider what you will need when you wake in the morning. Could you set the coffee pot to automatically brew? Lay out your clothes for the day? Pick up the kitchen so it's tidy for your morning? Whatever you can do tonight for your future self, she will thank you.

Set yourself up for success, and you will be so glad you did in the morning. And remember: His mercies are new with each rising sun. You don't have to do this perfectly, but you are fully capable of doing it consistently and truly changing the quality of your life in the process.

Emily's Ideal Evening Routine

After dinner: Pick up the kitchen and living room, turn down beds. Turn off overhead lights and turn on lamps. (We have these on a timer, and I love it!)

1: After tucking the kids in bed, I head downstairs to finish picking up.

2: A bath in the evening is my favorite. I use Epsom salt and plug my phone in my closet beforehand, usually around 7:00 p.m.

3: After my bath, I'll do my skincare routine, brush my teeth, and head to bed.

4: I love to read or watch a show before bed, so I'll spend a little time here.

5: Usually around 9:00 p.m. or so, I'll turn off the lights and drift off to sleep.

Sometimes, at the end of a long day, my brain just wants to get lost in an hourlong scroll on my phone. I do this sometimes, but when I do, I notice how frazzled or zoned out I feel afterward. Now I go to my closet and plug in my phone early in the evening to avoid this.

Sometimes a work or personal project will pop up and throw everything off course. This is fine. This is life.

EMILY'S IDEAL WEEKEND EVENING

On the weekends, Bryan and I will go on a date night, or we'll do something together as a family. Sometimes, we'll just lie low at home and cook a good meal together or watch football. Either way, weekends are about slowing down and loosening the reins on the schedule.

Acknowledgments

To Bryan, I love you. Thank you for always being there. Always cheering me up and cheering me on.

To Brady, Tyler, and Caroline. You are the light of my life. You are wonderfully made. I love you with all of me.

To Mom and Dad. Thank you for always reminding me what matters most. I love you and am grateful for your example.

To Team Simplified. Thank you for your endless dedication and unending friendship.

To my dearest friends. You know who you are. Thank you for always being by my side, for championing my books, and for being my village.

To my agent, Claudia, and my Thomas Nelson publishing team. Words will never be enough. Thank you for being my partners in this work. You are truly the best of the best.

About the Author

Emily Ley is the founder of Simplified®, a bestselling brand of planners and organizational tools for busy women found online and in Target, Walmart, Office Depot, and Staples.

She has spent nearly thirteen years empowering, inspiring, and equipping women in the areas of organization, planning, and simplicity. She is the host of The Simplified Podcast and author of national bestselling books *Grace, Not Perfection*; *A Simplified Life*; *When Less Becomes More*; and *Growing Boldly*.

Emily has been featured in *Forbes*, *Glamour*, and *Good Housekeeping* and was recently recognized as Entrepreneur of the Year by Studer Community Institute. She also serves on the board of advisors for the Rally Foundation for Childhood Cancer Research.

Now, as an author, podcaster, entrepreneur, wife, and mother, Emily lives in Pensacola, Florida, with her husband, Bryan, and their son Brady, and twins, Tyler and Caroline.

Put More Calm and Joy in Your Day

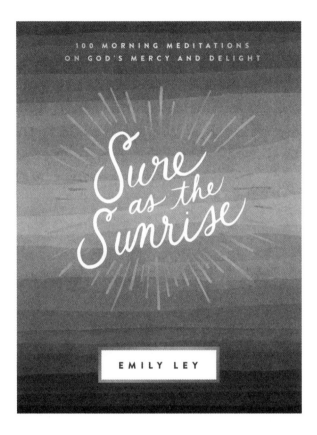

100 MORNING MEDITATIONS
ON GOD'S MERCY AND DELIGHT

Sure as the Sunrise

EMILY LEY

Do your days sometimes feel uncertain and chaotic? Do you wonder if what you're doing each day matters in the grand scheme of life? Are you seeking calm and peace amid turmoil? In *Sure as the Sunrise*, bestselling author Emily Ley offers inspiration and reassurance that God's mercy, delight, and provision are as sure as the sunrise— and ready to greet you each morning with hope and joy.

Give Space to What Matters Most

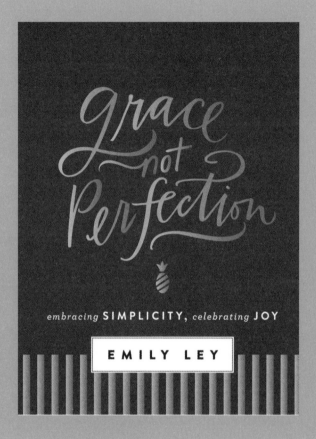

grace *not* Perfection

embracing **SIMPLICITY,** *celebrating* **JOY**

EMILY LEY

Have you been told you can have it all, only to end up exhausted and out of sorts with the people you love? Are you ready for a new way of seeing yourself—and your chaotic, beautiful life? Learn to live simply. Hold yourself to a more life-giving standard in *Grace, Not Perfection*, and allow that grace to seep into every part of your life.